WORLD HUNGER and SOCIAL JUSTICE

Gary E. McCuen

IDEAS IN CONFLICT SERIES

publications inc.

411 Mallalieu Drive
Hudson, Wisconsin 54016

Illustration & photo credits
ABCAP 104, Web Bryant 155, Rachel Burger 51, Carol & Simpson 161, Christian Child Care Inc. 35, Paul Conrad 127, DeOre 101, Joe Dombi 75, FAO 11, 15, 93, The Freeman 146, Horizons 47, 133, Marnie McCuen 87, Office of Technology Assessment 122, Mike Peters 169, Sack 109, 139, Sanders 31, David Seavey 61, 117, John Trever 103, Unesco Courier 67, World Bank 23

©1986 by Gary E. McCuen Publications, Inc.
411 Mallalieu Drive ● Hudson, Wisconsin 54016 ●
(715) 386-5662
International Standard Book Number 0-86596-055-0
Printed in the United States of America

CONTENTS

CHAPTER 5   HUNGER IN AMERICA

REASONING SKILL DEVELOPMENT

*These activities may be used as individualized study
guides for students in libraries and resource centers or as
discussion catalysts in small group and classroom
discussions.*

IDEAS
in CONFLICT ®

This series features ideas in conflict on political, social and moral issues. It presents counterpoints, debates, opinions, commentary and analysis for use in libraries and classrooms. Each title in the series uses one or more of the following basic elements:

Introductions that present an issue overview giving historic background and/or a description of the controversy.

Counterpoints and debates carefully chosen from publications, books, and position papers on the political right and left to help librarians and teachers respond to requests that treatment of public issues be fair and balanced.

Symposiums and forums that go beyond debates that can polarize and oversimplify. These present commentary from across the political spectrum that reflect how complex issues attract many shades of opinion.

A global emphasis with foreign perspectives and surveys on various moral questions and political issues that will help readers to place subject matter in a less culture-bound and ethno-centric frame of reference. In an ever shrinking and interdependent world, understanding and cooperation are essential. Many issues are global in nature and can· be effectively dealt with only by common efforts and international understanding.

Reasoning skill study guides and discussion activities provide ready made tools for helping with critical reading and evaluation of content. The guides and activities deal with one or more of the following:

RECOGNIZING AUTHOR'S POINT OF VIEW

INTERPRETING EDITORIAL CARTOONS

VALUES IN CONFLICT

WHAT IS EDITORIAL BIAS?

6

WHAT IS SEX BIAS?

WHAT IS POLITICAL BIAS?

WHAT IS ETHNOCENTRIC BIAS?

WHAT IS RACE BIAS?

WHAT IS RELIGIOUS BIAS?

From across *the political spectrum* varied sources are presented for research projects and classroom discussions. Diverse opinions in the series come from magazines, newspapers, syndicated columnists, books, political speeches, foreign nations, and position papers by corporations and non-profit institutions.

About The Editor

Gary E. McCuen is an editor and publisher of anthologies for public libraries and curriculum materials for schools. Over the past 14 years his publications of over 200 titles have specialized in social, moral and political conflict. They include books, pamphlets, cassettes, tabloids, filmstrips and simulation games, many of them designed from his curriculums during 11 years of teaching junior and senior high school social studies. At present he is the editor and publisher of the *Ideas in Conflict* series and the *Editorial Forum* series.

CHAPTER 1

WORLD HUNGER:
HISTORY AND OVERVIEW

THE CURRENT CRISIS: FACTS ON WORLD HUNGER

James Phillips

More than one billion people in the world are chronically undernourished. Between 700 million and 800 million people live on incomes insufficient to adequately secure the basic necessities of life.

Fifteen to twenty million people die each year of hunger-related causes, including diseases brought on by lowered resistance due to malnutrition. Three out of every four of these (75 percent) are children. Over 40 percent of all deaths in poor countries occur among children under five years old.

At least 100,000 children in Asia and Africa go blind each year from Vitamin A deficiency caused by inadequate diet. More than 500 million people in poor countries suffer from chronic anemia due to inadequate diet.

In wealthy countries, 12 to 15 out of every 1,000 newborn infants die before their first birthday. In poor countries, 100 out of every 1,000 newborns die before their first birthday.

The world currently spends an average of $550 billion a year producing, buying and selling military weapons. The world spends about $22 on military purposes for every dollar it spends on official development aid.

One out of every four human beings (25 percent) has no access to safe drinking water. In the 40 lowest income countries,

Reprinted from James Phillips, "World Hunger: Facts," *Oxfam America Education Publication*, pp. 1–3. James Phillips is a member of the Oxfam America staff.

fewer than 30 percent of the people have access to safe drinking water. In Ethiopia, for example, fewer than 6 percent of the people have regular access to safe drinking water, and most of that water is located some distance from where they live.

In Britain, there is one doctor for every 880 people. Nigeria has one doctor for every 44,620 people, while Ethiopia has one doctor for every 73,000 people. If someone in Britain gets sick, he/she shares the chance of getting a hospital bed with 100 other sick people. A Nigerian takes his/her chances with 2,410 other sick people.

What the world spends in half a day on military purposes could finance the entire malaria eradication program of the World Health Organization.

In 83 countries of the world, 3 percent of the landowners control almost 80 percent of the land. In Argentina, for example, 2 percent of the landowners own 75 percent of the land.

Less than 60 percent of the world's cultivable land is currently under cultivation. Less than 20 percent of the potentially cultivable land in Africa and Asia is under cultivation. Most of that land is controlled by large landowners or is open country.

The price of one military tank vehicle could provide classrooms for 30,000 students, or improved storage facilities for 100,000 tons of rice.

Two U.S.-based corporations control half of the world's wheat trade. One British corporation controls 80 percent of the world's production of cooking oils. Two North American companies control most of the world's production and supply of farm machinery and parts.

Thirty six of the world's 40 poorest countries export food to North America. Africa, where more than half the population suffers from chronic protein deficiencies, exports protein foods to Europe.

"When you rip aside the confusing figures on growth rates, you find that for almost two-thirds of humanity, the increase in income has been less than $1 a year for the last twenty years" (Mahbub ul Haq, Third World economist).

In the wealthy countries, 20 percent to 25 percent of the average family's income is spent on food. In most poor countries, the average rural poor family must spend as much as 75 percent to 85 percent of its income on food. In India, for example, the poorest 20 percent of the people spend as much as 85 percent of their income just to obtain food, but consume an average of fewer than 1,500 calories a day each (2,300 calories a day is the recommended minimum to maintain normal health and activity).

More than 800 million adults (more than half of the world's population) cannot read or write. Two-thirds of these illiterates are women.

10

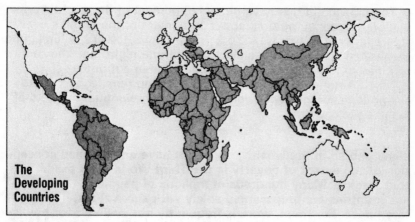

The Developing Countries

Source: FAO

Of all the children in poor countries now entering school, only one in five (20 percent) will complete the equivalent of eighth grade. Most of these will be male students.

The richest 20 percent of the people in 44 different countries consume 10 times what the poorest 20 percent of their fellow citizens consume. In Brazil, the rich consume 17 times more than the poor, and in South Africa, 29 times more.

One-half of one percent (0.5 percent) of one year's world military expenditures would pay for all the farm equipment needed to increase food production and approach self-sufficiency in food-deficit, low-income countries by 1990.

Everyday, the world produces two pounds of grain for every man, woman and child on earth. That is enough to provide everyone 3,000 calories a day, well above the recommended daily minimum of 2,300 calories.

The rich countries, including the United States, Western Europe, Japan and Australia, consume 70 percent of the world's food grains. Most of that is used to feed beef and dairy cattle.

In 1974, less than 20 percent of the grain which rich countries fed to their cattle would have entirely eliminated the grain shortages of the poor countries for that year. Although the United States dominates the world's rice trade, one-half (50 percent) of U.S. rice production goes directly into making breakfast cereals.

The average North American consumes 2,000 pounds of grain a year, but only about 150 pounds of that is consumed directly as grain or flour. The rest, 1850 pounds, is consumed as milk, eggs, meat and alcoholic beverages. The average Asian eats less than 400 pounds of grain a year, most of that in its original form of grain.

The poor countries have nearly 75 percent of the world's population, but consume only about 15 percent of the world's available energy. The two New York Trade Center tower buildings in Manhattan consume more electricity in one night than the capital cities of many poor countries consume in a month.

North Americans spend more on chewing gum, tobacco and alcoholic beverages each year than the entire annual budgets of many poor countries.

"Few people in the wealthy countries have any detailed conception of the extent of poverty in the Third World or of the forms that it takes. Many hundreds of millions of people in the poorest countries are preoccupied solely with survival and elementary needs. For them, work is frequently not available, or pay is low and conditions barely tolerable. Homes are constructed of impermanent materials and have neither piped water nor sanitation. Electricity is a luxury. Health services are thinly spread, and in rural areas only rarely within walking distance. Permanent insecurity is the condition of the poor. There are no public systems of social security in the event of unemployment, sickness or death of a wage earner in the family. Flood, drought or disease affecting people or livestock can destroy livelihood without hope of compensation. In the wealthy countries, ordinary men and women face genuine economic problems—uncertainty, inflation, the fear if not the reality of unemployment. But they rarely face anything resembling the total deprivation found in the poor countries. Ordinary people in the poor countries would not find it credible that the societies of wealthy countries regard themselves as anything but wealthy."

(From *North-South: A Program For Survival.* The report of the Independent Commission on International Development under the chairmanship of Willy Brandt.)

THE WORLD FOOD CONFERENCE

Theodor Galdi

The World Food Conference was convened in November 1974 as a response to a series of adverse occurrences that had affected world agricultural markets since 1972. It was a time of grave concern over future world food supplies. Chapter I of the assessment of the world food situation prepared by the staff of the Conference was entitled "The Food Crisis: Recent Developments." The chapter set out the series of circumstances that had led to sharply increasing prices for grain exports in 1972, 1973, and 1974. These included a 3 percent decline in global grain output between 1972 and 1973; large-scale Soviet grain purchases in 1972; failure of the anchovy catch off Peru; continuing drought in the Sahel and certain developing countries combined with flooding in others; synchronous economic boom periods in most of the developed countries causing increased prices for almost all commodities—including agricultural inputs; and successful supply management programs in certain developed countries.

The inter-relationship of all of these factors became manifest in prices. In January 1972, the U.S. wheat export price was $60 a ton. By January 1973, it had risen to $108 a ton, and in January 1974, it was $214 a ton. Similarly, the price of Thai rice rose from $131 a ton in January 1972 to $179 a ton in January 1973, reaching $438 a ton in January 1974. The peak of grain prices

Excerpted from *Feeding the World's Population,* a report by the U.S. House Committee on Foreign Affairs, October, 1984, pp. 3–7. Theodor Galdi is a specialist in international economics and foreign affairs.

coincided almost exactly with the opening of the World Food Conference. The consequences of these price increases varied considerably. The developed countries were effectively able to insulate their domestic markets from the effects of the price increases. The less developed countries (LDCs), however, were residual buyers in export markets and were, as a result, obliged to pay much higher prices for the food they did import.

The combination of declining agricultural output in the Third World and rising prices on international markets seemed, in the absence of corrective action, to threaten development plans of Third World countries and to presage increasing hunger in many parts of the less developed world. The plans for a world food conference grew out of these concerns. Twelve years have elapsed since planning for the Conference began, and ten since it was held. One important aspect of this study has been to compare actual developments since the Conference with projections that were made in the early 1970s.

Regional Food Overviews

An examination of the experience of the developing countries in feeding themselves since the early 1970s shows significant areas of improvement, though some parts of the world remain sources of concern. Sub-Saharan Africa is the only region in the world that has experienced actual declines in per capita food production in the last two decades. The current food situation in much of Africa gives cause for great concern. Drought, civil strife, and government mismanagement have all contributed to Africa's recent poor production record. Stagnant or declining production, combined with very high rates of population growth, have led to a need for increasing food imports. The need for food aid has increased because of a lack of foreign exchange. It appears that major changes will have to take place before a turnaround in the African food situation will be possible. In the meantime, substantial amounts of food aid will probably be needed.

Even though they have avoided the immediate major food problems of their southern neighbors, the experiences of the countries of North Africa are not particularly reassuring. Per capita food production in the recent past has been essentially flat. This, combined with increasing population, has led to substantial food imports—on both commercial and concessional terms.

In the 1981/82 crop year, Egypt and Algeria were the first and third largest non-Communist LDC importers of wheat in the world. While Algeria will most likely continue to be able to pay for needed food imports from oil and gas export revenue, the future ability of Egypt, Morocco and Tunisia to pay for increasing levels of food imports is uncertain.

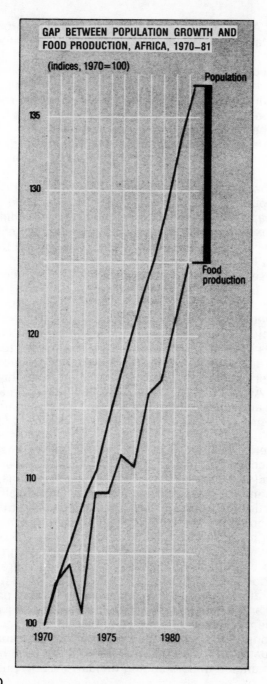

GAP BETWEEN POPULATION GROWTH AND
FOOD PRODUCTION, AFRICA, 1970–81

(indices, 1970=100)

Population

Food
production

Source: FAO

15

The great Asian population centers, chronically threatened in the past by famine, have avoided that specter. The near absence of the countries of South Asia as importers on world grain markets in the recent past is extremely gratifying for those who have been concerned about food supplies in this area. Though India, Pakistan, and Bangladesh received 1.4 million metric tons of cereal food aid in 1981, this was considerably less than the 4.2 million metric tons of food aid cereals needed in 1974. The initial impetus given by the Green Revolution to production in South Asia has been followed up with steps to maintain increasing output.

Defying the pessimistic projections of experts in the early 1970s, the countries of Southeast Asia have managed to increase per capita food production significantly. A willingness to pursue pragmatic agricultural policies has generally characterized the behavior of governments in this region, and these policies seem to have had substantial effects.

While these less developed Asian countries have generally done well in increasing food production, there is little ground for complacency. Malnutrition remains a severe and widespread problem. Even where population growth rates are declining, the number of mouths to feed is growing significantly. China and the countries of South and Southeast Asia will have to devote substantial resources to increasing agricultural production to sustain current nutritional levels, let alone improve them. Both the scale of Asian populations and the fluctuations in agricultural output are so great that one cannot rule out short-term requirements that would have major impacts on world food markets.

Latin America is a region of great contrasts. While a few of the smaller countries have experienced declines in per capita food production, all of the larger countries—Argentina, Brazil, Mexico, Colombia—have, in the recent past, increased per capita food production. In addition, U.N. statistics indicate that the proportion of people in Latin America suffering from some form of malnutrition has fallen from 50 percent in 1970 to 15 percent now. However, the effects of increasing population growth and urbanization will most likely place continuing pressure on Latin America's food resources.

In each major region, the resolution of a series of particular local issues and concerns will determine the prognosis for the future. While the less developed countries are the focus of the major portions of this study, the overall world food supply and demand situation—and its determinants—are crucial background elements in understanding the current LDC policy debate.

16

CHAPTER 2

WORLD HUNGER AND ECONOMIC GROWTH

WORLD HUNGER AND ECONOMIC GROWTH

OVERVIEW: POPULATION GROWTH AND ECONOMIC DEVELOPMENT

Population Crisis Committee

For nearly two decades technical and financial assistance to Third World population and family planning programs has been an important component of foreign aid programs. Support for these activities by the United States and other industrialized donors has been justified in part by the longstanding belief that rapid population growth in the developing world dilutes and in some cases impedes economic development.

But in the last several years this contention has been sharply challenged by a small group of Western economists who argue that population growth is often the driving force behind economic expansion and technological change. Citing historical precedents in Western countries and post-war economic successes in Japan, Taiwan, South Korea and elsewhere, they make three general points: first, that population growth is the natural result of improvements in the human condition, especially im-

Reprinted from "Population Growth and Economic Development," *Population,* February, 1985, p. 1. *Population* is a newsletter published by the Population Crisis Committee.

proved health; second, that an expanding labor force, an expanding market, and other consequences of population growth spur economic growth; and third, that economic progress, in and of itself, will lead to population stabilization through changes in desired family size. Direct interventions to reduce birthrates are unnecessary or even counterproductive.

In the United States this "anti-Malthusian" view, as it is called by its proponents, has recently gained support in some government circles and among political pressure groups (most prominently anti-abortion groups) who oppose assistance to population programs on other grounds. Their attack on U.S. population assistance peaked in the summer of 1984, during preparations for U.S. participation in the U.N. International Population Conference. It precipitated the first major public debate in the 20-year history of U.S. foreign aid for family planning. Although public and media attention declined after the Conference, the policy debate has continued.

At the heart of the debate is a singularly important but highly complex question. In today's less developed countries, where 90 percent of world population growth is occurring, does the need to adapt to population pressures contribute to greater economic innovation, increased investment, and more efficient exploitation of natural and human resources? Or do population pressures more often overload fragile economic and political institutions, impede capital formation just when more is needed, add to a pool of unproductive or unemployed labor, and contribute to the over-exploitation of scarce natural resources? Do demographic trends (up or down) influence economic performance in positive ways, in negative ways or not at all?

POPULATION GROWTH PROMOTES ECONOMIC DEVELOPMENT

Julian Simon

Julian Simon is a professor of economics and business administration at the University of Illinois, Urbana-Champaign, and is the author of The Economics of Population Growth. *The material appeared in somewhat different form in Mr. Simon's book* The Ultimate Resource, *which was published by Princeton University Press.*

Points to Consider

1. What does classical economic theory say about the results of population growth?
2. Why does the author believe that population growth may help, rather than hinder, economic development?
3. What is the most important benefit that population growth confers on an economy?
4. How is the ultimate resource on the planet defined?

Julian Simon, "World Population Growth," *The Atlantic Monthly,* August, 1981, pp. 70–76.

The evidence does not confirm the conventional theory. It suggests that population growth almost certainly does not hinder, and perhaps even helps, economic growth.

Every schoolchild seems to "know" that the natural environment is deteriorating and that food is in increasingly short supply. The children's books leave no doubt that population size and growth are the villains. In the *Golden Stamp Book of Earth and Ecology* we read: "If the population continues to explode, many people will starve. About half of the world's population is underfed now, with many approaching starvation. . . . All of the major environmental problems can be traced to people—more specifically, to too many people." But these facts, which are reported to children with so much assurance, are either unproven or wrong.

The demographic facts, to the extent that they are known, are indeed frightening, at first glance. The human population appears to be expanding with self-generated natural force at an exponential rate, restrained only by starvation and disease. It seems that, without some drastic intervention to check this geometric growth, there will soon be "standing room only." . . .

Zero Population Growth

Although no one knows what population size or rate of growth the future holds in store, one often hears that zero population growth, or ZPG, is the only tolerable state. Classical economic theory bolstered this conviction. It purports to show that population growth inevitably reduces the standard of living. The heart of all economic theory of population, from Malthus to *The Limits to Growth,* can be stated in a single sentence: The more people using a stock of resources, the lower the income per person, if all else remains equal. This proposition derives from what economists have called the law of diminishing returns. Two men cannot use the same tool, or farm the same piece of land, without producing less than they would if they did not have to share. A related idea is that two people cannot nourish themselves as well as one person can from a given stock of food. The age distribution that results from a high birthrate reinforces this effect; the number of children in proportion to workers will be larger. Also, the more children women have, the less chance they have to work outside the home, so the work force is diminished further.

21

According to this reasoning, both sheer numbers of people and the age distribution that occurs in the process of getting to the higher numbers ought to have the effect of a smaller per capita product. But the evidence does not confirm the conventional theory. It suggests that population growth almost certainly does not hinder, and perhaps even helps, economic growth.

One piece of historical evidence is the concurrent explosion of population and economic development in Europe from 1650 onward. Further evidence comes from a comparison of the rates of population growth and output per capita in those developed countries for which data are available for the past century. No strong relationship between the two variables appears. For example, population has grown six times faster in the United States than in France, but the rate of increase in output per capita has been about the same. The populations of Great Britain and Norway grew at the same pace for the past century, but the rate of Norway's output per capita was about a third faster. Australia, on the other hand, had a very fast rate of population growth, but its rate of increase in output per capita was quite slow.

Studies of recent rates of population growth and economic growth are another source of evidence. In less-developed countries, per capita income has been growing as fast as or faster than in the developed countries, according to a World Bank survey for the years 1950 to 1975, despite the fact that population has grown faster in developing countries than in developed countries.

Such evidence does not show that fast population growth in developed countries *increases* per capita income. But it does contradict the belief that population growth inevitably *decreases* economic growth. The lack of a cause-and-effect relationship between population and economic growth has a number of explanations, as follows:

—People make special efforts when they perceive a special need. For example, American fathers work extra, the equivalent of two to five weeks a year, for each additional child. In the long run, this yearly 4 to 10 percent increase in work may fully (or more than fully) balance the temporary loss of labor by the mother. (The other side of this coin is that people may slack off when population growth slows and demand lessens.)

—The larger proportion of young people in the labor force which results from population growth has advantages. Young workers produce more in relation to what they consume than older workers, largely because the older workers receive increases in pay with seniority, regardless of productivity. And because each generation enters the labor force with more education than the previous generation, the average worker becomes more and more knowledgeable.

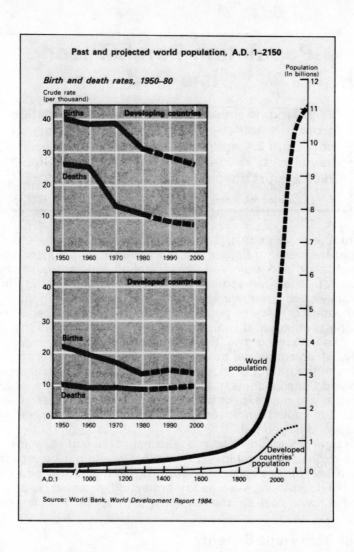

Past and projected world population, A.D. 1–2150

Birth and death rates, 1950–80

Crude rate (per thousand)

Population (In billions)

Developing countries

Births

Deaths

Developed countries

Births

Deaths

World population

Developed countries' population

Source: World Bank, *World Development Report 1984.*

—Population growth creates business opportunities and facilitates change. It makes expansion investment and new ventures more attractive, by reducing risk and by increasing total demand. For example, if housing is overbuilt or excess capacity is created in an industry, a growing population can take up the slack and remedy the error.

—More job opportunities and more young people working mean that there will be more mobility within the labor force. And mobility greatly enhances the efficient allocation of resources: the best matching of people to jobs.

—Population growth promotes "economies of scale": the greater efficiency of larger-scale production. Through this mech-

23

Population Bomb Theory Is a Dud

Taking the world as a whole, population growth is actually falling—to 2 per cent a year now from 2.4 per cent in the 1960s. The decline has already rendered the figures in the Global 2000 Report obsolete.

Lawrence W. Reed, *Human Events,* February 2, 1985

anism, the more people, the larger the market, and therefore the greater the need for bigger and more efficient machinery, division of labor, and improved transportation and communication. Hollis B. Chenery, an economist, compared manufacturing in less-developed countries and found that, all else being equal, if one country is twice as populous as another, output per worker is 20 percent larger. It is an established economic truth that the faster an industry grows, the faster its efficiency improves. One study, which compared the output of selected industries in the U.S. with the output of those same industries in the United Kingdom and Canada, showed that if you quadruple the size of an industry, you may expect to double the output per worker and per unit of capital employed. This should hold true for the developed world in general.

A larger population also provides economies of scale for many expensive social investments that would not be profitable otherwise—for example, railroads, irrigation systems, and ports. And public services, such as fire protection, can also be provided at lower cost per person when the population is larger.

Most Important Benefit

All of the explanations just summarized have economic force, but the most important benefit that population growth confers on an economy is that people increase the stock of useful knowledge. It is your mind that matters economically, as much as or more than your mouth or hands. In the long run, the contributions people make to knowledge are great enough to overcome all the costs of population growth. This is a strong statement, but the evidence for it seems strong as well. . . .

What is the connection between innovation and population size and growth? Since ideas come from people, it seems reasonable that the number of improvements depends on the number of people using their heads. This is not a new idea. William Petty wrote in 1683 that "it is more likely that one ingenious curious man may rather be found out amongst 4 millions than 400 persons." Hans Bethe, who won the Nobel Prize for physics in 1967, has said that the prospects for nuclear fusion would be rosier if the population of scientists were larger. Bethe said, "Money is not the limiting factor. . . . Progress is limited rather by the availability of highly trained workers."

Even a casual consideration of history shows that as population has grown in the last century, there have been many more discoveries and a faster rate of growth in productivity than in previous centuries. In prehistoric times, progress was agonizingly slow. For example, whereas routinely we develop new materials—say, plastics and metals—millennia passed between the invention of copper metallurgy and of iron metallurgy. If population had been larger, technological discoveries would surely have come along faster. Ancient Greece and Rome have often been suggested as examples contrary to this line of reasoning. Therefore, I plotted the numbers of great discoveries, as recorded by historians of science who have made such lists, against Greek and Roman populations in various centuries. This comparison showed that an increase in population or its rate of growth (or both) was associated with an increase in scientific activity, and population decline with a decrease.

In modern times, there is some fairly strong evidence to confirm the positive effect of population growth on science and technology: in countries at the same level of income, scientific output is proportional to population size. For example, the standard of living in the U.S. and in Sweden is roughly the same, but the U.S. is much larger than Sweden and it produces much more scientific knowledge. A consideration of the references used in Swedish and U.S. scientific papers and of the number of patented processes that Sweden licenses from the U.S. bears this out.

Why isn't populous India a prosperous and advanced country? I have not argued that a large population will by itself overcome all the other variables in a society—its climate, culture, history, political structure. I have said only that there is no evidence to prove that a large population *creates* poverty and underdevelopment. India is poor and underdeveloped for many reasons, and it might be even more so if it had a smaller population. The proper comparison is not India and the United States but India and other poor countries, and the fact is that India has one of the largest scientific establishments in the Third World—perhaps in part because of its larger population. . . .

Conclusion

In the short run, all resources are limited: the pulpwood that went into making this magazine, the pages the magazine will allow me, and the attention the reader will devote to what I say. The longer run, however, is a different story. The standard of living has risen along with the size of the world's population since the beginning of recorded time. There is no convincing economic reason why these trends toward a better life should not continue indefinitely. Adding more people causes problems, but people are also the means to solve these problems. The main fuel to speed the world's progress is our stock of knowledge, and the brake is our lack of imagination. The ultimate resource is people—skilled, spirited, and hopeful people—who will exert their wills and imaginations for their own benefit, and so, inevitably, for the benefit of us all.

POPULATION GROWTH INCREASES HUMAN MISERY

Russell W. Peterson

Russell W. Peterson is the President of the National Audubon Society. The following comments are excerpted from a speech at Carleton College in Northfield, Minnesota.

Points to Consider

1. How does the author define the term "ostrichism"?
2. Why has the population bomb not been defused?
3. What is meant by the term "ecological carrying capacity"?
4. Why is there hope and what should be done?

Reprinted from a speech by Russell W. Peterson at Carleton College, March 29, 1985.

There are signs in many parts of the world today—Ethiopia is only one of many places, a tip of the iceberg—that we Homo sapiens are beginning to exceed the carrying capacity of our planet.

There's a movement afoot to brand anyone who sounds the alarm over present global trends as a doomsayer and a fear-monger and an un-American wimp. The title of a recent book tells us: "The Good News is the Bad News is Wrong."

Population explosion? No problem, say the self-styled optimists. The more the merrier. With twice as many people in the world, we'll have twice the technological know-how. Resource depletion? No problem, they assure us. With our ingenuity for extracting and synthesizing, we will never run out of anything we need. Pollution? Not to worry. Just unburden industry from all the environmental regulations and then just watch unfettered free enterprise clean up our air, land and water. . . .

It's my contention that this simple-minded view of things is not real optimism but ostrichism. It is sticking one's head in the sand instead of confronting reality head-on, as true optimists do. . . .

The Population Bomb

Contrary to what you may have read or heard, the global population bomb has not been defused. Though the rate of population growth has declined somewhat in recent years, the number of human beings is increasing more rapidly than ever.

In 1984, world population grew by 84 million, more than ever before. By the year 2000, human population is expected to be growing by 100 million a year. That's almost 20 Minnesotas a year—but with a big difference. Some 90% of this growth in human numbers will occur in places that bear not the remotest resemblance to this prosperous, pleasant state. It will occur mostly in the spreading urban slums and depleted countrysides of Third World nations, places where hunger and malnutrition are the norm, where housing, medical facilities and education are, to put it mildly, inadequate.

In the past 10,000 years, human populations have reached or exceeded the carrying capacity of their local or regional environments many times. And human societies have sometimes paid the price of a population collapse. But now, in just a few decades, our species has begun to strain the limits of the global bi-

28

ological systems that support all life—the oceans, grasslands, croplands, wetlands and forests. We human beings are consuming the earth's productive resource base at the same time that our growing numbers require *more* resources. We are spending our biological capital.

Aside from the threat of nuclear war, population growth is the most pressing environmental issue of our times. Almost every environmental problem, almost every social and political problem as well, either stems from or is exacerbated by the growth of human population.

The population trends that have become clearly visible in the second half of this century are without historical precedent. Think of this. It took Homo sapiens a million years or so to reach a population of one billion. That happened about 1830. The second billion was added during the next 100 years—we passed that milestone when I was starting high school. Now the world is adding its fifth billion in just 13 years.

During the last decade, the overall population growth *rate* has turned downward. For the world as a whole, growth peaked at 2.1 percent in the second half of the 1960s. Estimated annual growth for the early 1980s is about 1.7 percent.

This decline in the rate of population growth has led many observers to believe that the world in general, and most individual countries as well, no longer face serious population problems.

The reality is, however, that the momentum from decades of rapid population growth will continue far into the future. The momentum will continue even in many countries where replacement level fertility has already been achieved. This is because of the large number of young people already born who have yet to reach child bearing age. Moreover, in much of Africa and South Asia, and in some countries of Latin America, no measurable or significant drop in fertility has yet occurred.

According to the World Bank, the population of India will nearly double in the next 45 years. That will make India one-third larger in terms of people than China is today. Bangladesh by the same time will have tripled and will have 266 million people jammed into an area the size of Wisconsin. Mexico, which today has the most rapidly growing labor force—much of it unemployed—of any large country in the world, will more than double in size. And in Kenya, where 17 million people are now putting heavy pressure on the limited supply of arable land, the population will *quintuple!*

When Robert McNamara was president of the World Bank, he coined the term "absolute poverty" to characterize a condition of life so degraded by malnutrition, illiteracy, violence, disease and squalor, to be beneath any reasonable definition of human decency. In 1980, the World Bank estimated that 780 million persons in the developing countries lived in absolute poverty. That's about three times as many people as live in the entire United States.

As Mr. McNamara will not (and should not) let us forget, a major concern raised by poverty of this magnitude lies in the physical and intellectual impairment of children. Parental investments of both money and time are critical in the early years of development if a child is to reach its full potential. But in many countries the great majority of children are born into absolute poverty—and so they are handicapped from the start.

Millions of these children receive insufficient protein and calories to permit optimal development of their brains. Additional millions die each year, before they are five years old, from diseases stemming from malnutrition. For many of those who do live, the capacity to learn is reduced. A culture of poverty is being transmitted down the generations, sacrificing human resources and impeding social progress.

Ecological Carrying Capacity

This seems an appropriate place to say something about the ecological principle of carrying capacity.

As any wildlife biologist knows, once a species reproduces itself beyond the carrying capacity of its habitat, natural checks and balances come into play. The species that breeds excessively will inevitably experience what biologists call a die-back or population crash. The human species is governed by this same natural law. And there are signs in many parts of the world today—Ethiopia is only one of many places, a tip of the iceberg—that we Homo sapiens are beginning to exceed the carrying capacity of our planet.

It is important that we be aware of what's happening to the earth's basic biological systems. Until world population reached three billion in 1960, the yield of these systems expanded more rapidly than population. At that point, however, the margin began to narrow. Global population growth outstripped forest production after 1964. Since 1970, the fish catch per person has fallen by 13 percent. As world population passed four billion, grasslands production of beef, mutton and wool began to fall behind population growth.

Overfishing, overgrazing, and overcutting of forests have now become widespread.

In Kenya, for example, not only is rapid population growth causing increased human misery, but Kenya's superb wildlife is being extinguished by human poaching and habitat loss. There's no way around it—people have to eat.

Madonna and Child

By Bill Sanders, © by and permission of News America Syndicate.

In Haiti, soaring population has clearly surpassed the country's carrying capacity. Most of Haiti's trees have been cut down without being replaced. Much of the country's topsoil has washed away. The male unemployment rate is about 50%. Large numbers of Haitians, aptly described as "ecological refugees," have been forced to leave their homeland.

Largely because of illegal immigration from the increasingly crowded countries of Latin America, the United States has the fastest growing population of any industrial nation. We are currently adding about two-and-a-half million people each year—the equivalent of a new California every decade.

We, the wealthy minority must learn to use resources far more efficiently. And we must move rapidly to stabilize our own population. Both steps are fundamental in helping to bring the world's people and resources into equilibrium. . . .

Conclusion

During his debate with Walter Mondale, President Reagan asserted that "the population explosion, if you look at actual figures, has been vastly exaggerated." At the United Nations Population Conference last summer in Mexico City, an Administration spokesman dismissed global population growth as a "neutral phenomenon." And one of Mr. Reagan's population advisers, Julian Simon, recently declared that "we should cry not with worry and sadness, but with enthusiasm and joy, at the increasing number of people."

This bizarre, head-in-the-sand attitude sounds like something straight out of Alice in Wonderland. It would almost be comical if the problem, and the Administrations' response to it, were not fraught with tragedy.

Today, as happened yesterday and will happen again tomorrow, 40,000 children will perish. Tonight, 400 million children will go to bed—if they have a bed—with empty stomachs. Right now, in Brazil alone, 11 million abandoned children, nearly three times the population of this entire state, are living in the streets.

In spite of these dire statistics, there *is* hope! That is why I am an optimist.

Thanks to the efforts of many developing countries with financial support from donors such as the U.S., hundreds of millions of couples are now practicing family-planning.

Studies show that most other couples in developing nations also wish to limit the size of their families. Given the knowledge and the wherewithal, these couples too will practice birth control. And when the enormous unmet demand worldwide for family-planning services is met, there will no longer be the need, as is true today, for 40 million couples to terminate their unwanted pregnancies by abortion each year.

International family-planning should be supported as never before if we are to move toward a more stable world and a decent quality of life for all people. We here in the U.S. must get the Congress to debate and reverse the President's decision and to increase its contribution for family-planning appreciably. Ignorance, ideology, and mindless optimism must not be allowed to hinder this all-important effort.

5 READING

ON THE THRESHOLD OF DISASTER

The Global 2000 Report to the President

This Global Report was a response to President Jimmy Carter's directive to the Council on Environmental Quality and the Department of State to make a one year study of the probable changes in the world's population, natural resources and environment through the end of the century.

Points to Consider

1. How many people may be desperately poor in the year 2000?
2. What might cause the impoverishent of many people?
3. What are the population projections for the year 2000?
4. What steps are recommended to prevent a major global catastrophy?

"Major Findings and Conclusions", *The Global 2000 Report to the President,* Vol. I, April, 1981, pp. 1–5.

Life for most people on earth will be more precarious in 2000 than it is now—unless the nations of the world act decisively to alter current trends.

If present trends continue, the world in 2000 will be more crowded, more polluted, less stable ecologically, and more vulnerable to disruption than the world we live in now. Serious stresses involving population, resources, and environment are clearly visible ahead. Despite greater material output, the world's people will be poorer in many ways than they are today.

For hundreds of millions of the desperately poor, the outlook for food and other necessities of life will be no better. For many it will be worse. Barring revolutionary advances in technology, life for most people on earth will be more precarious in 2000 than it is now—unless the nations of the world act decisively to alter current trends.

This, in essence, is the picture emerging from the U.S. Government's projections of probable changes in world population, resources, and environment by the end of the century, as presented in the Global 2000 Study. They do not predict what will occur. Rather, they depict conditions that are likely to develop if there are no changes in public policies, institutions, or rates of technological advance, and if there are no wars or other major disruptions. A keener awareness of the nature of the current trends, however, may induce changes that will alter these trends and the projected outcome.

Principal Findings

Rapid growth in world population will hardly have altered by 2000. The world's population will grow from 4 billion in 1975 to 6.35 billion in 2000, an increase of more than 50 percent. The rate of growth will slow only marginally, from 1.8 percent a year to 1.7 percent. In terms of sheer numbers, population will be growing faster in 2000 than it is today, with 100 million people added each year compared with 75 million in 1975. Ninety percent of this growth will occur in the poorest countries. . . .

World food production is projected to increase 90 percent over the 30 years from 1970 to 2000. This translates into a global per capita increase of less than 15 percent over the same period. The bulk of that increase goes to countries that already have relatively high per capita food consumption. Meanwhile per capita consumption in South Asia, the Middle East, and the less devel-

34

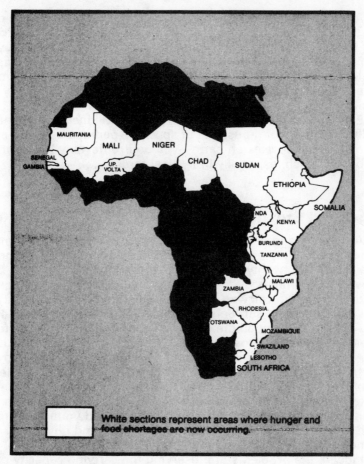

MAURITANIA
MALI
NIGER
SENEGAL
GAMBIA
UP.
VOLTA
CHAD
SUDAN
ETHIOPIA
SOMALIA
NDA
KENYA
BURUNDI
TANZANIA
MALAWI
ZAMBIA
RHODESIA
OTSWANA
MOZAMBIQUE
SWAZILAND
LESOTHO
SOUTH AFRICA

White sections represent areas where hunger and food shortages are now occurring.

Source: Christian Child Care, Inc.

oped countries (LDCs) of Africa will scarcely improve or will actually decline below present inadequate levels. At the same time, real prices for food are expected to double.

Arable land will increase only 4 percent by 2000, so that most of the increased output of food will have to come from higher yields. Most of the elements that now contribute to higher yields—fertilizer, pesticides, power for irrigation, and fuel for machinery—depend heavily on oil and gas. . . .

Serious deterioration of agricultural soils will occur worldwide, due to erosion, loss of organic matter, desertification, salinization, alkalinization, and waterlogging. Already, an area of cropland and grassland approximately the size of Maine is becoming barren wasteland each year, and the spread of desertlike conditions is likely to accelerate.

Atmospheric concentrations of carbon dioxide and ozone-depleting chemicals are expected to increase at rates that could alter the world's climate and upper atmosphere significantly by 2050. Acid rain from increased combustion of fossil fuels (especially coal) threatens damage to lakes, soils, and crops. Radioactive and other hazardous materials present health and safety problems in increasing numbers of countries.

Extinctions of plant and animal species will increase dramatically. Hundreds of thousands of species—perhaps as many as 20 percent of all species on earth—will be irretrievably lost as their habitats vanish, especially in tropical forests. . . .

Projected Growth Rates

At present and projected growth rates, the world's population would reach 10 billion by 2030 and would approach 30 billion by the end of the twenty-first century. These levels correspond closely to estimates by the U.S. National Academy of Sciences of the maximum carrying capacity of the entire earth. Already the populations in sub-Saharan Africa and in the Himalayan hills of Asia have exceeded the carrying capacity of the immediate area, triggering an erosion of the land's capacity to support life. The resulting poverty and ill health have further complicated efforts to reduce fertility. Unless this circle of interlinked problems is broken soon, population growth in such areas will unfortunately be slowed for reasons other than declining birth rates. Hunger and disease will claim more babies and young children, and more of those surviving will be mentally and physically handicapped by childhood malnutrition.

Indeed, the problems of preserving the carrying capacity of the earth and sustaining the possibility of a decent life for the human beings that inhabit it are enormous and close upon us. Yet there is reason for hope. It must be emphasized that the Global 2000 Study's projections are based on the assumption that national policies regarding population stabilization, resource conservation, and environmental protection will remain essentially unchanged through the end of the century. But in fact, policies are beginning to change. In some areas, forests are being replanted after cutting. Some nations are taking steps to reduce soil losses and desertification. Interest in energy conservation is growing, and large sums are being invested in exploring alternatives to petroleum dependence. The need for family planning is slowly becoming better understood. Water supplies are being improved and waste treatment systems built. High-yield seeds are widely available and seed banks are being expanded. Some wildlands with their genetic resources are being protected. Natu-

Ecological Roots of Famine

Desertification is the destruction or diminution of the biological potential of the land, which can lead to desert-like conditions. It is one aspect of the widespread modern deterioration of ecosystems, and has reduced or destroyed the land's capacity for plant and animal production at a time when increased productivity is needed to support growing populations. Important factors in contemporary society—the struggle for development and increased food production, attempts to adapt and apply modern technologies, population growth and demographic change—interlock in a network of cause and effect.

Ruth Sillman, *Peace & Freedom*, May–June, 1985

ral predators and selective pesticides are being substituted for persistent and destructive pesticides.

Encouraging as these developments are, they are far from adequate to meet the global challenges projected in this Study. Vigorous, determined new initiatives are needed if worsening poverty and human suffering, environmental degradation, and international tension and conflicts are to be prevented. There are no quick fixes. The only solutions to the problems of population, resources, and environment are complex and long-term. These problems are inextricably linked to some of the most perplexing and persistent problems in the world—poverty, injustice, and social conflict. New and imaginative ideas—and a willingness to act on them—are essential.

The needed changes go far beyond the capability and responsibility of this or any other single nation. An era of unprecedented cooperation and commitment is essential. Yet there are opportunities—and a strong rationale—for the United States to provide leadership among nations. A high priority for this Nation must be a thorough assessment of its foreign and domestic policies relating to population, resources, and environment.

The United States, possessing the world's largest economy, can expect its policies to have a significant influence on global trends. An equally important priority for the United States is to cooperate generously and justly with other nations—particularly in the areas of trade, investment, and assistance—in seeking solutions to the many problems that extend beyond our national boundaries. There are many unfulfilled opportunities to cooperate with other nations in efforts to relieve poverty and hunger, stabilize population, and enhance economic and environmental productivity. Further cooperation among nations is also needed to strengthen international mechanisms for protecting and utilizing the "global commons"—the oceans and atmosphere. . . .

Conclusion

With its limitations and rough approximations, the Global 2000 Study may be seen as no more than a reconnaissance of the future; nonetheless its conclusions are reinforced by similar findings of other recent global studies that were examined in the course of the Global 2000 Study. All these studies are in general agreement on the nature of the problems and on the threats they pose to the future welfare of humankind. The available evidence leaves no doubt that the world—including this Nation—faces enormous, urgent, and complex problems in the decades immediately ahead. Prompt and vigorous changes in public policy around the world are needed to avoid or minimize these problems before they become unmanageable. Long lead times are required for effective action. If decisions are delayed until the problems become worse, options for effective action will be severely reduced.

THE INCREASING ABUNDANCE
OF RESOURCES

David Osterfeld

*Dr. David Osterfeld is Associate Professor of Political
Science at St. Joseph's College, Rensselaer, Indiana.*

Points to Consider

1. What is meant by the term "catastrophism"?
2. Who is Paul Ehrlich and what predictions did he make?
3. Why are resources becoming more abundant?
4. Why is the human mind the ultimate resource?
5. Why are some nations poor and others wealthy?

David Osterfeld, "The Increasing Abundance of Resources", *The Freeman,* June, 1984, pp. 360–76.

Herman Kahn and Associates have concluded that 99.9 percent of the world demand is for metals whose supply is either "clearly" or "probably inexhaustible."

The year 1980 marked the publication of *The Global 2000 Report to the President.* The *Report,* which is the joint product of the Council on Environmental Quality, the Department of State and eleven other government agencies, is only slightly less pessimistic than the *Limits to Growth* published in 1972. . . . The fact that the major conclusions of *The Limits to Growth* are endorsed by the *Global 2000 Report* is significant. Since *The Global 2000 Report* is the joint product of no less than 13 government agencies this means that the catastrophist position has received the government's official stamp of approval.

Not only is catastrophism the official position of the government, it is also the prevailing viewpoint—in fact usually the only viewpoint—found in either educational textbooks or the more popular press. . . .

Catastrophism: Predictions and Realities

Of course catastrophism in one form or another is really nothing new. It can be traced back at least to 1798 with the publication of Thomas Malthus' *Essay on Population.* Since that time we have been fed a steady diet of catastrophist predictions of imminent disaster. The most revealing thing about these predictions is that they have never come true. . . .

It is noteworthy that the predictions of today's catastrophists have proven no more accurate. In his dramatic 1969 article, "Eco-catastrophe," noted biologist Paul Ehrlich made his predictions for the decade of the 1970s. Among other things Ehrlich predicted (1) "increasing poverty" and world hunger. In fact, he said, "some ten to twenty million will starve to death this year (1969)"; (2) the rapid deterioration of the "raw material situation"; (3) the reduction of life expectancy to 42 years by 1970; (4) the "end of the ocean" by 1979, and (5) "the birth of the Midwestern desert," scheduled for the summer of 1973. It is, says Ehrlich, "a pretty grim scenario." Yet is is "based on projection of trends already appearing." "We're a long way into it already."

Fortunately, events have turned out quite differently. The United Nation's Food and Agriculture Organization began collecting data on world food production in 1948. The data indicate

40

that between 1948 and the present, *per capita* food output has increased by 40 percent, or just over one percent per year. And data compiled by the United States Department of Agriculture presents a picture even slightly rosier. In other words, in contrast to the catastrophist predictions of Ehrlich and others, both FAO and USDA data demonstrate that world food supply has consistently outstripped population increases. Put differently, the data clearly show that the world food situation is improving, not deteriorating. . . .

Resources: Increasing Abundance

The most revealing *fact* about resources is that for over the past one hundred years their prices, in real terms, have fallen. This suggests that their supply is growing, not diminishing. And this, in fact, is the case. A study prepared for the President of the United States by the Council on International Economic Policy disclosed that the "known reserves" or stocks of eleven out of twelve important metals have, despite growing consumption, actually increased over the twenty year period from 1950–70. Iron reserves grew by 1,321 percent, Potash by 2,360 percent and Phosphates by 4,430 percent.

Similar conclusions were reached by Earl Cook. "Despite large increases in consumption over the past 40 years," Cook concludes, "we now have many more 'years' of lead reserves than we did 40 years ago, as well as about 25 percent more years of copper and zinc reserves. . . . There is currently an over-supply of both copper and crude oil in the world, and the supply of ores of iron and aluminum despite enormous increases in the production and consumption of both during the past 50 years, seem almost boundless." Clearly, the *predictions* and *expectations* of the Chicken Little Gang are directly counter to the basic *facts* of the resource situation. But how is such a thing possible? Resource consumption has increased enormously during the twentieth century. How, then, can it be that our supply of resources, instead of diminishing, has actually expanded?

The catastrophist view of resources is *static.* There is, they believe, a fixed amount of oil, copper or natural gas, and the more of these stocks we consume, the less there is left. That the supply of resources is finite is a very plausible notion. It is also wrong.

Technological advances permit us to utilize existing resources more efficiently. For example, in 1900 the lowest grade of copper ore economically mineable was about 3.0 percent. Today, the cutoff point has fallen to 0.35 percent. Similarly, while much of the coal closest to the earth's surface has already been extracted, advances in mining technology have actually reduced

TABLE 3: HOW "KNOWN RESERVES" ALTER

Ore	Known Reserves in 1950 (1,000 Metric Tons)	Known Reserves in 1970 (1,000 Metric Tons)	Percentage Increase
Iron	19,000,000	251,000,000	1,321
Manganese	500,000	635,000	27
Chromite	100,000	775,000	675
Tungsten	1,903	1,328	−30
Copper	100,000	279,000	179
Lead	40,000	86,000	115
Zinc	70,000	113,000	61
Tin	6,000	6,600	10
Bauxite	1,400,000	5,300,000	279
Potash	5,000,000	118,000,000	2,360
Phosphates	26,000,000	1,178,000,000	4,430
Oil	75,000,000	455,000,000	507

SOURCE: Council on International Economic Policy, Executive Office of the President, *Special Report, Critical Imported Materials* (Washington, D.C.: U.S. Government Printing Office, December 1974).

the cost of obtaining coal despite having to go much deeper to extract it. . . .

The results of these improved methods are as significant as they are astounding. Economist Wilfred Beckerman, using data supplied by the World Bank, has calculated that the stock of metals in the top mile of the earth's crust is sufficient "to last about one hundred million years." Herman Kahn and Associates have concluded that 99.9 percent of the world demand is for metals whose supply is either "clearly" or "probably inexhaustible." Very similar conclusions were reached by W. D. Nordhaus. "The clear evidence," he concludes, "is that the future will not be limited by sheer availability of important materials." This includes energy. "With only current technology" Nordhaus says, "there are resources for more than 8,000 years at the current rate of consumption." Allowing for technological advances during this time, "there is virtually unlimited energy available." In short, the prospect of "resource depletion" is not a matter of decades, as the Chicken Little Gang would have us believe, but it lies hundreds, probably thousands of years in the future.

But even this prospect, distant as it is, is without foundation. For not merely does technology enable us to find and use existing resources more efficiently, it also enables us to create new resources by discovering uses for previously worthless materials. Oil is only the most dramatic example. Prior to the nineteenth century oil was a liability and land known to possess this slimy ooze was worth very little. It was only with the dawn of the machine age that oil became a resource. But while technology creates resources, it must be borne in mind that technology itself is created by the human mind, which Julian Simon has aptly dubbed the ultimate resource. As Thomas Sowell has written,

> A natural resource is something occurring in nature that *we know how to use* for our purposes. Our knowledge is as integral to the concept of a natural resource as the physical thing itself. An inventory of natural resources two centuries ago would not have included uranium or hydroelectric power, because no one knew how to use such things. Once resources are seen in this light it no longer follows that there are fewer natural resources with the passing centuries.

While the supply or stocks of given physical *materials* is, in some ultimate sense, finite, the "stock" of human knowledge is not. And this is the crux of the matter. Since the human mind creates resources, this means that the supply of resources is not finite but is limited only by the "stock" of knowledge. And since this "stock" has been increasing rather than running out, it should come as no surprise that the supply of "physical resources" has also been expanding. As one writer recently put it, to worry about running out of resources is very much like worrying that, because there is a finite number of musical notes, we are in danger of "running out" of music.

Governments, Markets, Poverty and Prosperity

The foregoing is merely meant to demonstrate that "resource depletion" is not limiting economic growth. It is not meant to imply that everything is splendid. There are of course many people and societies which continue to exist on the verge of starvation. While this is tragic, it has little to do with resources.

It is often forgotten that the developed countries of today were not always developed. Until only recently all nations were

43

"undeveloped." It was only in the eighteenth century, in what is now termed the "Industrial Revolution," and only in a particular part of the world, in what is designated as the "West," that the standard of living began to rise above the subsistence level. Even today poverty is the rule for the great bulk of mankind, wealth the *exception.* Thus, the real question is not why most nations are poor but why some are wealthy. That is, what made possible the dramatic transformation of one small section of the world while conditions elsewhere remained practically unchanged? ...

In brief, what is required to overcome poverty and hunger is really quite simple: economic freedom. All the resources in the world will not produce economic growth in its absence. Conversely, the single most significant factor in perpetuating poverty is excessive regulation of individual behavior. While this may take the form of social custom, such as communal land tenure or the caste system in India, government regulation is no doubt more important.

For example, as everyone knows, post-war China has suffered from "overpopulation" and has taken rather extreme measures to reduce its growth. What is not so well known is that its population was growing by only two percent a year, which was actually *below* the world's average during this time. China's problem was that due to government mismanagement, food production between 1950 and the mid-1970s either remained stable or actually declined. It has only been since the death of Mao that the "socialist" experiment has been largely abandoned and agricultural output has increased.

Elsewhere in the Third World government policies such as minimum wages, state-created monopolies, tariffs in excess of 100 percent, and widespread nationalizations, have frightened off investors, both domestic and foreign, thus impeding economic growth. ...

Conclusion

The widespread belief in the prospect of imminent resource depletion is unfounded. The supply of resources is actually expanding, not diminishing. While such maladies as poverty and hunger may in fact worsen in the future, the tragedy is that they are likely to be caused by the very thing the Chicken Little Gang sees as the solution to the mythical problem of resource depletion: more government controls and regulations.

GLOBAL ECONOMIC GROWTH WILL IMPROVE THE HUMAN CONDITION

Andrew Young

Andrew Young is the Mayor of Atlanta, Georgia and a former U.S. Ambassador to the United Nations under the Carter administration. He was a prominent leader in the civil rights movement.

Points to Consider

1. What factors have led to world hunger?
2. Why is hunger no longer just a problem of nature?
3. What is meant by international economic development and how would it help reduce hunger?
4. Why would the establishment of a global development fund be an initial step in reducing hunger?

Andrew Young, "World Hunger and Global Development," *Presbyterian Survey,* March, 1985, pp. 2–3.

The eradication of global hunger can happen; it will happen, but only in the context of overall world development and advancement.

Food is scarce in the developing world only because there is no effective mechanism to transfer the necessary resources and technology from the wealthy nations to the hungry nations.

Hunger has resulted not only from drought and increasing landlessness. A scarcity of jobs and capital, brought about by worldwide recession and the Third World's mounting debts to developed nations, is the major cause of today's and tomorrow's malnutrition and starvation.

Modern Era

In our era of modern technology and transportation, hunger is no longer simply a problem of nature, but a problem of economics. Only an economic solution can offer long-term hope to the hundreds of millions who are undernourished.

The solution, I believe, lies in new concepts for international economic development. Developing countries desperately need economies that are expanding, not contracting; they need projects to provide jobs for the unemployed and underemployed; they need foreign exchange to import agricultural technology and basic foodstuffs.

These preconditions to eliminating hunger can only exist if Third World economies are developing rapidly and equitably.

Given the frightening state of the world economy—an $800 billion Third World debt, soaring interest rates and growing protectionism in the industrialized world—and the limited success of the existing development institutions, it is easy to dismiss global development as just another pipe dream. A Civil Rights Act in the United States was once considered another pipe dream, as was peaceful independence for Zimbabwe. Global development can also be a success story, but some bold and imaginative steps must be taken.

A Global Fund

An initial step should be the establishment of a global development fund designed to spur development throughout the world. The fund would provide the necessary capital for 10 or 20 major infrastructure projects worldwide. Priority would be given

46

Source: Horizons, 1984

to those projects that would have an impact on an entire region, such as a sea-level Panama Canal, a manmade lake in central Africa, or a massive hydraulic power plant in South America.

The fund would serve as a type of global stimulus providing jobs, foreign exchange and training to the developing world, and markets, jobs and eventually export earnings to the industrialized world.

Such a fund would receive its capital contributions from private sources. There is a great deal of capital floating around international markets, but it is only being turned over in a paper economy. This capital could be harnessed for constructive uses in a global development fund through industrialized government tax and investment incentives. The use of private funds would alleviate many of the political problems the World Bank and the International Monetary Fund encounter in obtaining sufficient contributions from industrialized governments.

The construction of 10 or 20 regional infrastructure projects would have immediate and important effects on the international economy. It would be a major first step toward making the dream of global development a reality.

I believe the once unthinkable proposition of eliminating hunger would quickly become a very real possibility.

Contributing to Growth

When I first spoke to you 3 years ago, I asked that we examine the terrible shocks inflicted upon the world economy during the 1970s, that all of us face up to the origins of those problems and also recognize our ability to withstand and surmount them.

For our part, we said one conclusion seemed both undeniable and universally true. The societies whose economies had fared best during these tumultuous times were not the most tightly controlled, not necessarily the biggest in size, nor even the wealthiest in natural resources. What united the leaders for growth was a willingness to trust the people—to believe in rewarding hard work and legitimate risk.

So the United States made a new beginning—one based on our conviction that we could only meet the challenge of contributing to world economic growth and of assuring that all countries, especially the poorest, participate fully in that growth by renouncing past policies of government—of government regimentation and overspending—and by taking decisive action to get our domestic house in order and restore incentives to liberate the genius and spirit of our free people.

President Reagan in a speech to the World Bank, September 25, 1984.

The eradication of global hunger can happen; it will happen, but only in the context of overall world development and advancement.

8

WORLD HUNGER AND ECONOMIC GROWTH

HUMAN NEEDS, NOT ECONOMIC GROWTH, ARE THE REAL PROBLEMS

Marolyn McDiarmid

Marolyn McDiarmid participated in an Oxfam study tour to Sri Lanka last summer. She is a Quaker and works as assistant coordinator of the home-delivered meal program of the Greater Minneapolis Council of Churches.

Points to Consider

1. How are the terms "Sarvodaya" and "Schramadana" defined?
2. What subjects were discussed at the village meeting?
3. How is "Sarvodayan self-reliance" explained?
4. How are the "Sarvodaya Schramadana" ideas about economic and social life different from Western nations' ideas about commercial progress and making money?

Marolyn McDiarmid, "Sarvodaya Schramada Movement", *Global Perspectives,* March–April, 1985, pp. 1–3.

Sarvodayan self-reliance is knowing what needs to be done to obtain basic needs, unity of community, quality of life, and completeness of spirituality.

Sarvodaya, a self-development movement, signifies the awakening or liberation of "one and all." The movement's saying, "Sabbe satta sukhi hontu," means "may all beings be well and happy." It reflects a Buddhist wish for welfare for all of the people. Believing national development should begin with the villages, the movement helps people organize themselves to deal directly with their own problems. Since 1958 Sarvodaya has become active in about 30 percent of the 23,000 villages on the island, with programs in health, education, agriculture and local industry. An estimated two-and-a-half to three million islanders have experienced the impact of this movement.

I and other participants in the Oxfam America study tour had spent one week at two Sarvodayan centers, one in Moratowa, near the capital of Columbo, the other in Anuradhapura, sacred city and ancient capital in the north central province. Resource people at both centers had carefully explained the history, philosophy, programs and future visions of the movement. Impressed with the deep commitment of Sarvodaya staff and movement volunteers for the welfare of the island's people, I was eager to see the application of such ideals.

The Sarvodayan philosophy is carried out in the days of Shramadana. "Shrama" means "labor" and "dana" means "to give." Today, a Shramadana, a sharing of labor, would find villagers and the six Americans of the study tour group transforming development philosophy into human reality. Work!

We washed quickly at the well, brushed our teeth in the yard for lack of a bathroom or even a latrine, rolled up bamboo sleeping mats, milked the cows, ate breakfast, swept the yard and gathered up the ancient style work tools that would earn us blisters by the day's end.

Then the family's father returned home from a night in a small hut on stilts in the rice paddy watching for wild elephants. The men of the village took turns executing the farming detail of elephant chasing on the farm cooperative. If elephants broke out of the jungle into the rice fields the man on guard was to toss large firecrackers at them to chase them back into the jungle.

Despite little sleep, P.B., the father, washed, ate and joined us. He was the village school principal and knew others would look to him for leadership today. As the road began to fill with peo-
50

Rachel Burger

ple emerging from small side trails, we joined them to walk to the work site. Only the very young and old would stay behind to prepare our mid-morning break of water, tea and bread.

A Village Meeting

We gathered in front of the village shrine, where their Lord Buddha smiled benevolently. Removing our thongs, we formed a large circle inside the sacred ground area. Short prayers were said for the coming work day, and a prayer flag, Buddhist flag and Sarvodaya banner were raised onto bamboo poles. As a

51

group, we now headed for the trail encircling the 2000-year-old tank, a water reservoir the size of a large lake, which was built by ancient kingdoms for irrigation and water supply.

Rapid jungle growth demanded continuous clearing if there was to be access to the tank. The tank is the center for many activities vital to village life, including clothes washing, bathing, harvesting of lotus flowers for food and offerings to the Buddha shrines, and collecting cooking and drinking water.

The Shramadana had been decided earlier in the week at a village meeting. When a village requests assistance from Sarvodaya, villagers are instructed in how to organize the village internally so all can participate in the decision making. All villagers are invited to attend the meetings. This group then becomes the primary planning body for identifying village problems and developing solutions.

The meeting had been held under shade trees in the center of the village. Women sat on one side and men on the other. The village monk sat in the only chair, facing the people. He was a startling figure with his brilliant tangerine orange sarong and shaven head. His presence was a reminder to adhere to spiritual principles during the discussion and decision making process.

The women were active and respected participants in the meeting. At first, many of the men wanted only to clear the tank trail. However, the female teacher spoke vigorously and relentlessly for the school yard to be cleared also. Another woman wept while pleading for a fence to be mended that would keep the cows from wandering into her chili field and trampling the plants. It was an energetic discussion, almost heated at times. Then everyone grew silent. Consensus came quietly and quickly. A committee would be dispatched to see to the cow problem, the morning would be spent clearing the tank trail, the afternoon given to the school yard.

Amazing! Was I in Kattamurichana or back home at a Quaker business meeting? These third world rural villagers had just held a meeting with everyone participating, had come to consensus instead of voting, and made use of silence to find the "sense" of the meeting. The last amazement was to hear a closing statement from the school principal. He asked that we not isolate or reject a person who had done a wrong deed. Instead, we were to continue to see him as a friend, speaking to him only of that act that had been wrong. A different kind of development model? Indeed. This meeting was markedly different from a typical stateside city council project meeting.

We began our work at the trail leading to the water tank. I was hacking at the thick tangled roots on a sloping jungle bank with a broad sharp hoe. Alongside both banks, villagers bent to the labor. Those without tools waited on the trail for work rotation. . . .

A heavy rain at midday prevented the completion of the Shramadana. I accompanied two teenage girls to the shelter of the preschool and helped take blood samples from villagers for malaria testing. The women had volunteered to train at the Sarvodaya Center in Anuradhapura in the malaria program. They now visit area villages performing the testing. Later, at tea in their family hut, I observed the family pride for these daughters. A village over 1000 years old, with a population infected with malaria at a 50 percent rate, receives health care not from light-skinned Europeans or North Americans, but from its own people. This form of self-development fosters roots of self-worth and confidence in their own culture and allows for ownership and commitment to village programs.

Keystone Principle

Self-reliance is a Sarvodaya keystone principle. Sarvodaya self-reliance is not defined in the usual western sense of making our way monetarily nor is it like my definition which means paying taxes and waiting for city or state to clear my "access trails." Rather, Sarvodayan self-reliance is knowing what needs to be done to obtain basic needs, unity of community, quality of life, and completeness of spirituality. They then actively work to achieve these things. Their sense of self-reliance also includes an understanding of the inter-connectedness of people, where values and spirituality need to be addressed and included in any goal.

Community self-reliance was evident in this Shramadana. Villagers had seen the problem of trail overgrowth and proceeded to clear their own access trails. Other days they would hold

Shramadanas with neighboring Sarvodaya villages to build common roads, dig wells, erect shared clinics or schools, all basic societal infrastructures. The Sarvodaya message to uneducated, isolated, poor villagers is: "You have the abilities and intelligence to meet your own needs according to your wishes and priorities. Gather together, identify the problems, decide collectively the resolutions and act together to accomplish your goals." Sarvodaya then stands ready to give assistance and any training that is requested. The message doesn't wait for governments to decide if the people need or deserve services. It encourages the approximately three million Sarvodayan members to draw strength from their cultural and spiritual roots and to work in respectful unity to provide for their own needs.

The similarity between this Buddhist-based development program message and the message of Christian base communities in Latin America is striking. Both speak out to the immediate condition of the people and support self-efforts to effect change. Could it be that the Universal Spirit is passing the word along to poor and oppressed people throughout the world that their time is now, and that they deserve lives of well-being and self-respect?

Dr. A. T. Ariyaratna, founder of Sarvodaya, speaks of "awakening" the people. The challenge lies in awakening a people living in 2000-year-old lifestyles and bringing them safely and holistically into a technical and competitive world where spiritual and cultural values are frequently pushed aside for marketplace profits and personal gain. Four hundred fifty years of colonial rule left the majority of Sri Lankans with a colonial mentality of dependency and undeservedness. Sarvodaya's gift is its full comprehension of these complexities, its vibrant and strength filled spiritual base and its compassionate love for the people.

COMPARING CULTURAL VALUES

This activity may be used as an individualized study guide for students in libraries and resource centers or as a discussion catalyst in small group and classroom discussions.

A. **Conflicting Economic Values**

Examine carefully the two competing economic systems presented below. Then go on to part B.

Economic System One	Economic System Two
1. Promotes the philosophy of personal gain as the path to satisfaction and happiness.	1. Promotes the philosophy of satisfying basic needs of the whole society.
2. Places great importance on material abundance found in industrial societies.	2. Promotes life styles founded on simple agricultural and production methods which are not dependent on great material wealth.
3. Promotes development of large scale industrial projects requiring huge capital investments.	3. Encourages small cooperative projects under local control.
4. Stresses need for foreign loans and capital investment to promote industrial development.	4. Advocates a philosophy of economic independence to help relieve the nation from foreign debt and foreign political pressures.
5. Places high value in the growth of large complex cities that attract people from rural areas.	5. Promotes the development of the agrarian economy so people will not relocate in large urban centers.
6. Promotes competition and the pursuit of material wealth and economic growth and advancement.	6. Encourages cooperation rather than competition as a means of meeting basic needs.

B. Reaching a Consensus

Working as individuals or in small discussion groups, read through the following statements and evaluate each one as indicated.

Mark A for any statement with which you agree.
Mark D for any statement with which you disagree.
Mark N for any statement you are not sure about.

_____1. Economic system one offers the best way for rich nations to organize their economic order.
_____2. Economic system two offers the best way for poor nations to organize their economic order.
_____3. The major problem with economic system one is that too much pollution results from material abundance.
_____4. The values in system two will never raise people out of poverty and suffering in poor nations.
_____5. The values and goals in system one are adhered to by wealthy elites in most poor nations who control vast wealth, while the poor masses suffer and die from lack of necessary food, medicine, shelter and work.
_____6. The most feasible economic system for any nation would be a combination of the best values in both economic systems one and two.

C. Points to Consider

1. What elements of economic system one do you like the best? The least?
2. What elements of economic system two do you like the best? The least?
3. What advantages would economic system one have for poor nations? What would be the disadvantages?
4. What advantages would economic system one have for rich nations? What would be the disadvantages?
5. What advantages would economic system two have for poor nations? What would be the disadvantages?
6. What advantages would economic system two have for rich nations? What would be the disadvantages?

CHAPTER 3

HUNGER AND FOREIGN RELATIONS

FOREIGN AID PROMOTES
THIRD WORLD HUNGER

Francis Moore Lappé, Joseph Collins, and
David Kinley

*Francis Moore Lappé and Joseph Collins founded the
Institute for Food and Development Policy in 1975. The
Institute specializes in the study of world food problems
in poor nations. Before joining the Institute for Food and
Development Policy, David Kinley researched for two New
York based organizations that study the influence of U.S.
multinational organizations in Latin America.*

Points to Consider

1. What "new directions" do U.S. policy makers claim to follow?
2. What is the real cause of poverty and hunger?
3. Why does foreign aid increase the level of poverty and hunger?
4. Under what circumstances should foreign aid be withheld?
5. When might it be wise to offer economic assistance to a country?

Francis Moore Lappé, Joseph Collins and David Kinley, *Aid as Obstacle:
Twenty Questions about Our Foreign Aid and the Hungry,* Institute for
Food and Development Policy (San Francisco, 1981) pp. 9–14.

We are calling for a halt to all economic and military support for governments controlled by narrowly based elites which use repression to protect their interests and to block the demands of their own people for redistribution of control over productive assets.

"They are poor and hungry. We in the United States have so much. Shouldn't we increase our foreign aid?" . . .

Justifying their programs, aid spokespersons assure us that strategies for development have dramatically improved, and that emphasis on rapid industrialization and the "green revolution" has been discarded in favor of a new development strategy. The new "basic human needs" approach, we are told, directly focuses on the poor—the productivity of small farms, small-scale technology, and infrastructure that will help the entire rural population in third world countries.

U.S. aid policymakers testify that they follow the "new directions" reforms mandated by Congress. According to former Secretary of State Cyrus Vance, the principal purpose of U.S. development assistance programs is "to meet the basic needs of the poor people in the developing countries." Since most of the world's nearly one billion underfed people live in rural areas, aid is now directed, we are told, to agriculture and rural development. It is also claimed that food aid programs are also designed to directly benefit the poor and contribute toward self-sufficiency. We are assured, moreover, that U.S. aid has been linked to human rights in recipient countries to encourage more democracy and less repression.

Appropriate Terminology?

Along with the "new directions" thrust of major U.S.-funded aid programs has come catchy new terminology to describe it. Today, we hear much about "integrated rural development," "appropriate technology," "popular participation," "raising small farm productivity" and "self-reliance." But whatever the terminology, our foreign assistance programs will help the poor and hungry abroad only if they attack the root causes of their suffering. Since "root causes" has itself become a popular phrase— sometimes used glibly—we must be very precise about what we mean.

Our research at the Institute for Food and Development Policy leads us to conclude that the cause of hunger and rural poverty is *not* overpopulation, scarcity of agricultural resources, or lack of modern technology. Rather, *the root cause of hunger is the increasing concentration of control over food-producing resources in the hands of fewer and fewer people.* Privileged elites preempt control over food-producing resources for their own benefit. No new combination of material inputs, no matter how "appropriate," can address the powerlessness of the poor that is at the root of hunger. (We document these findings in detail in our book *Food First: Beyond the Myth of Scarcity* (Ballantine Books, 1979).)

Aid Reinforces Power Relationships

Field investigations and other research have led us to realize that U.S. foreign assistance fails to help the poor because it is *of necessity* based on one fundamental fallacy: that aid can reach the powerless even though channeled through the powerful. Official foreign assistance necessarily flows through the recipient governments, and too often (particularly in those countries to which the United States confines most of its aid) these governments represent narrow, elite economic interests. We have learned that additional material resources are usually not needed to eliminate hunger. In fact, the influx of such outside resources into those countries where economic control is concentrated in the hands of a few bolsters the local, national and international elites whose stranglehold over land and other productive resources generates poverty and hunger in the first place. Instead of helping, we *hurt* the dispossessed majority.

Tubewells designed to benefit the poorest farmers in a Bangladesh village become the property of the village's richest landlord; food-for-work projects in Haiti intended to help the landless poor end up as a boon to the village elite; rural electrification justified as a prerequisite to jobs in rural industries results in the elimination of jobs for thousands of poor rural women in Indonesia.

Foreign aid, we have found, has not transformed antidemocratic economic control by a few into a participatory, democratic process of change. It cannot. Rather, official foreign aid *reinforces* the power relationships that already exist. Certainly this is the case with government-to-government aid. Only with great difficulty can private ("voluntary") agencies sometimes avoid the same dynamics.

Aid policymakers claim that they are now focusing on the poorest countries and on those governments demonstrating commitment to the poor. In this book we challenge both claims. Our research shows instead that the bulk of our aid flows not to the countries with the greatest poverty, but to those with some of the world's most narrowly based and repressive regimes. We challenge the claim that most new aid projects target poor peo-

ple. Most funds actually go to large-scale infrastructural projects benefitting the better-off people who control land and marketing systems and have political influence. Finally, we contend that even the few projects which do promote the productivity of small farmers (and perhaps boost their productivity), still fail to address the real sources of their poverty. Moreover, such projects hurt the poor rural majority—the landless and nearlandless.

Lack of Resources or Lack of Power?

Some might interpret us to be saying that the aid establishment is not living up to its rhetoric. But that is only part, and not the most important part, of what we are saying. What we are saying is that U.S. government aid and agencies such as the World Bank cannot ally themselves with the poor, in part because the definition of the problem of poverty reflected in their projects is wrong.

The prevailing diagnosis of why people are poor and hungry is that they have been "left out" of the development process. From this diagnosis flows one solution—bring the poor *into* development. "Basic needs" aid strategies are conceived as a way to widen the development process to include the poor. But such a diagnosis is simply another version of the fallacious theory that one can reach the poor by expanding a process controlled by the rich.

A very different diagnosis is that rather than being *left out* of the development process, the poor have been an integral part of the process—both as resource and as victim. The poor have provided their labor, their products and often their land. The issue, then, is not to bring the poor into the development process, but for the poor to achieve the power they need to direct a development process in their interests.

The official aid agencies' diagnosis is that the poor are poor because they lack certain things—irrigation, credit, better seeds, good roads, etc. But we ask: *Why* are they lacking these things? In studying country after country, it becomes clear that what the poor really lack is *power,* power to secure what they need. The aid agencies focus on the lack of power. Therein lies the fundamental difference.

By identifying the problem as a lack of resources, official aid seeks to bring in what is lacking locally. We have found that not only are the needed resources often available locally, but also that the outside resources—brought in by official aid—invariably end up in the hands of elites who are then even better able to usurp the labor and dwindling resources of the poor majority.

The official diagnosis assumes that the poor are living in a static condition of backwardness and that the role of aid is to offer material incentives and benevolent prods to get things moving. But in countries where so many people are poor and hungry, the reality in the villages and in the nation is this: if positive change is not already under way, it is because of people's legitimate fear of those more powerful and because of the constraints on production built into hierarchical, often quasi-feudal social structures.

While prevailing development theory sees stagnation and backwardness in third world countries, the truth is that in every country where many are poor and hungry, people are working to achieve genuine development, beginning with redistribution of control over land. To some, their efforts appear insignificant in light of the mighty forces against them. But recall that many observers belittled the freedom movements in the African Portuguese colonies as late as the early 1970s, and those of the Nicaraguan people as late as 1979. Likewise, observing the suffering

Remove the Obstacles

If aid is not the answer, what can we do? We can begin working now to remove the obstacles in the way of third world people working for change. For Americans, that means cutting off U.S. aid to governments that shut their citizens out of control over resources and changing the policies of banks that lend money to the South African government or corporations that sell computers to the Guatemalan police. That means working to educate other Americans so that we can all work for a world in which everyone has the right to eat. These actions would ensure real national security for us all.

"Biting the Bullet," *Food First Action Alert,* Institute for Food and Policy Development, February, 1984.

of so many Chinese in the 1940s, knowledgeable Americans suggested that a high death rate in China might be humane, since the country could never feed itself. Who would say that today?

With all the obstacles they face, these societies and others serve to highlight the most important lesson of development—the need to first address the question of control over productive resources. . . .

Why a Push for More Aid?

To ally themselves with the interests of the poor, agencies such as U.S. AID would have to support those groups throughout the third world that are confronting the issue of power—the issue of control over resources. To do so would pit these agencies against the interests of the elites dominating most governments in the world today. To do so would go headlong against the formidable lobbyists of multinational corporations. To do so would be to risk supporting democratic economic alternatives abroad that might lead more Americans to question how just their own economic system has become. Obviously, no U.S. government agency is about to do so. This is why we conclude that agencies of the U.S. government are incapable of arriving at a correct diagnosis of the root causes of hunger—a diagnosis that puts control over resources in the central position.

The promotion of the wrong diagnosis permits many well-intentioned persons (including some within aid agencies) to be used by the real beneficiaries of foreign aid—multinational cor-

porations and their third world partners—who are the most
trenchant lobbyists for foreign aid.

The Role of Outsiders

From these contrasting analyses of the problem of hunger
and poverty flow very different roles for the outsider. Our government tells us that the appropriate role for the United States is
to supply needed resources and help maintain "stability" in the
third world. Mounting economic and military aid to countries
like the Philippines and El Salvador is so justified. But if progress will come only with redistribution of control over productive
resources, then outside interventions to maintain "stability" will
only postpone the day when that necessary progress can begin.
Moreover, by bolstering the forces that block change, outside
support makes brutal and bloody confrontations even more inevitable.

Our definition of the problem leads to a very different challenge to those outside the third world. We should not try to
make our aid agencies live up to their new rhetoric. This would
only contribute to the problem by reinforcing the notion that
U.S. foreign aid can help in countries where control over resources is tightly concentrated. Once we understand that government-to-government aid cannot transform power relationships, but can only reinforce what exists, it becomes clear that
we must work to limit such aid to countries where there is already under way a fundamental restructuring of decision-making
power.

Remove the Obstacles

Many who have called for a halt or reduction in U.S. foreign
aid have actually been saying, "Cut them off. Let them solve
their own problems. We must take care of our own." This is not
what we are saying. Rather, we are calling for a halt to all economic and military support for governments controlled by narrowly based elites which use repression to protect their interests
and to block the demands of their own people for redistribution
of control over productive assets. Such a move would mean cutting off those governments now most favored by U.S. economic
assistance and military aid. Our thesis is that these economic
and military supports actually block efforts by those who are
working for a more just sharing of control over resources. As
Americans, our responsibility is to remove such obstacles. At the
same time we must work to make our own society truly democratic and self-reliant so that one day it might play a constructive
role around the world.

10

HUNGER AND FOREIGN RELATIONS

FOREIGN AID NEEDED IN HUNGER FIGHT

Jean Mayer

Dr. Jean Mayer is the president of Tufts University and the former vice chairman and acting chairman of the Presidential Commission on World Hunger. He is an internationally recognized expert in the field of nutrition.

Points to Consider

1. What record has the U.S. had on aid to hungry nations?
2. How many people suffer from malnutrition?
3. What specific recommendations are made for different ways to give foreign aid?
4. What kind of agricultural assistance should be given by the U.S. to needy nations?

Reprinted from testimony by Dr. Jean Mayer before the House Committee on Agriculture, July 23, 1981.

65

It is very much in the interest of the United States to make the elimination of hunger and malnutrition a major focus of our relationships with the developing world.

I am particularly pleased that these hearings are being held because they renew my hope that something will be done to conquer hunger and malnutrition in the world. This, and nuclear proliferation, are the two most serious and urgent problems we face. Hunger and malnutrition among the most vulnerable groups in developing nations sow the seeds of chaos in our global village, and they are not inevitable. There is no question that we have the ability and the technology to feed both the 4.5 billion people who are on earth today and the 1.8 billion who will be added by the year 2000. The question is whether we have the compassion, the enlightened self-interest, and the will and can develop the necessary organization to do it.

The U.S. Record

Until the last decade the United States has had a proud record of aid to hungry nations. In the case of each initiative against hunger, both here and abroad, a bipartisan coalition in the Congress took the lead, carrying out the effort in cooperation with the Executive branch. I think of Point Four and Food for Peace, the hearings in the House and Senate that led to the First White House Conference on Food, Nutrition and Health and the action to end hunger in America, of the later Senate Conference on a National Nutrition Policy, that began, if late in the day, an exploration of means to end hunger in the world, an exploration that was continued by the recent Presidential Commission on World Hunger that was also bipartisan, also mandated by the Congress.

The membership of the Commission represented a wide range of interest and experience. Dr. Borlaug was a member. So were Senators Dole and Leahy, Representatives Gilman and Nolan. So were Harry Chapin and John Denver. A number of committed people worked very hard. There were points on which we did not agree, but we were able to arrive at the beginning of a national consensus on what to do about world hunger.

Unfortunately, this is one presidential commission that, so far as I am aware, has had no impact whatever on the consciousness of the previous administration, the Congress, or the nation.

In recent conversations I have had with Western European statesmen, they have expressed concern and alarm at the fact

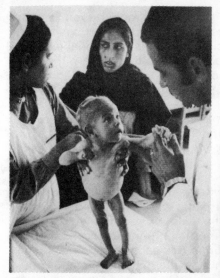

Above, a child before and after treatment at the UNRWA (United Nations Relief and Works Agency for Palestine Refugees in the Near East) Khan Younis Rehydration Nutrition Centre, Gaza Strip. Reprinted from the *Unesco Courier*, April, 1984.

that while we now have a coherent East-West policy, indeed a very forceful one, the United States has no North-South policy. There is no better way to begin than with an attack on world hunger and malnutrition.

You have asked me particularly to speak as a nutritionist. It would be helpful to define what it is that we are facing and its parameters.

Famine and Malnutrition

Not a year goes by that there is not a famine or acute food shortage somewhere in the world. The hunger of famine—starvation—is sadly easy to identify. It is the face of the starving children of Cambodia, Somalia, the Sahel. It is fearsome and devastating. When starvation is used as a weapon against innocent noncombatants in war or civil conflict, it is indefensible. Fortunately, there is now an international effort under way to try to outlaw the use of famine as a weapon. But famine can at least be attacked straightforwardly. It occurs in a definable area and has a finite duration. So long as there is food available somewhere, relief agencies can deal with the crisis; sometimes they can even prevent it.

Malnutrition, on the other hand, is a chronic condition that affects a far larger proportion of the human race, but is harder to

67

define and attack. Its treatment involves not mobilization to combat a crisis but long-term actions to prevent one—actions that affect economic and social policies as well as nutritional and agricultural ones. In the background is always the concern that too rapid an increase in population combined with a failure to keep pace in food production will give rise to massive famines that cannot be controlled.

Malnutrition may come about in several ways. A person may not get enough food, which is undernutrition. A diet may lack one essential nutrient or more, giving rise to deficiency diseases such as pellagra, scurvy, rickets, goiter, or the blindness that is caused by vitamin A deficiency. There may be a condition or an illness, either genetic or environmental, that prevents the digestion of food or absorption of nutrients, which is secondary malnutrition. Finally, a person may be taking in too many calories or consuming an excess of one or more components of an otherwise-reasonable diet. Malnutrition in this sense of overnutrition is a disease of affluent people in both the rich and the poor nations. . . .

Children with a chronic protein deficiency grow more slowly and are small for their age. In severe deficiency growth stops altogether. The spectrum of protein-calorie malnutrition varies, from a diet that is relatively high in calories and deficient in protein (the syndrome known as Kwashiorkor) to one that is low in both calories and protein (called marasmus).

Although protein-calorie malnutrition is the most prevalent form of undernourishment, diseases caused by deficiencies of specific vitamins or minerals are also widespread. The prevalence of certain of the classic deficiency diseases has decreased since World War II; beriberi is now rare and the acute form of pellagra has essentially been eradicated. By contrast, blindness caused by a lack of vitamin A occurs in over 100,000 children every year, and with particular frequency in India, Indonesia, Bangladesh, Vietnam, the Philippines, Central America, northeastern Brazil, and parts of Africa. Goiter, resulting from an iodine deficiency, is common in remote inland regions, in central Africa, and the mountainous regions of South America and the Himalayas. . . .

The human beings most vulnerable to the ravages of malnutrition are infants, children up to the age of five or six, pregnant and lactating women, and the elderly. For the infant, protein in particular is necessary during fetal development for the generation and growth of bones, muscles and organs. The child of a malnourished mother is more likely to be born prematurely or small and is at greater risk of death or of permanent neurological and mental dysfunction.

Growing children, pound for pound, require more nutrients

68

than do adults. A malnourished child is more susceptible to the common childhood diseases, and illness in turn makes extra demands on nutritional reserves. . . .

In my judgment, it is reasonable to set the number of people suffering from malnutrition at 400 to 500 million and to add to that another billion or more who would benefit from a more varied diet. The largest concentration of these people is in Asia, Southeast Asia and sub-Saharan Africa. Malnutrition, wherever it exists, is most severe among infants, preschool children, and pregnant and nursing women. It is most prevalent in depressed rural areas and the slums of great cities. The problem is lack of calories as much as lack of protein; where calories tend to be adequate, protein tends to be adequate too. Although a lack of food is the ultimate factor in malnutrition, that lack results from a number of causes, operating alone or in combination. A nation may lack both self sufficiency in food production and the money to buy food or to provide the farm inputs necessary to increase production. The poorer members of the population may lack income to buy the food that is available, and regional factors, like customs in child feeding and restrictions on the movement of supplies, may prevent the food from getting to the people who need it the most.

The single most important cause of malnutrition is the prevalence of poverty in the majority of developing countries. . . .

Three Fronts

It is very much in the interest of the United States to make the elimination of hunger and malnutrition a major focus of our relationships with the developing world. To do this, we must move on three fronts.

First, and for some years to come, there will be the need for food aid in crisis areas like Cambodia and Somalia, and in some chronically food-short areas with very primitive agriculture, such as parts of sub-Saharan Africa. Except in emergencies, however, this aid should be given with attention to protecting indigenous food production; otherwise it is counter-productive. With U.S. surpluses piling up there may be a tendency to think more about food aid than agricultural assistance.

Second, we can encourage and support with technical assistance the drive toward national self-sufficiency in food production in developing lands. This means not only help in adapting techniques of the Green Revolution, but also aid in industrial development, particularly of those activities that are adjuncts to agriculture and food production and distribution, provided they are also labor-intensive.

Programs for Hunger

The major function of the Taskforce is to encourage U.S. policies and programs which alleviate hunger. The Taskforce views the alleviation of hunger and its eventual eradication as one of the most pressing moral and ethical issues of our time. We find it morally indefensible that hundreds of millions of people now suffer from hunger and malnutrition in a world which has the resources to provide an adequate diet for everyone.

Interreligious Task Force on U.S. Food Policy, August 10, 1981.

Finally, because the Green Revolution is energy-intensive we must move strongly ahead with research on alternative methods of agriculture and food production, including aquaculture, that can be put in place by the year 2000. It is one of mankind's great tragedies that the nations which most need this research and the trained personnel to apply it do not have the knowledge or resources to develop either.

Specific Recommendations

Specifically, I would like to offer the following recommendations to the members of this Committee, as a beginning in addressing the problem:

To ensure that development assistance goes to the countries and people who need it most and ensure that it is as effective as possible, the United States should:

1. give more authority about development-related decisions to the Director of the International Development Authority.

2. immediately double the level of U.S. development assistance. The aim should be to give 0.7 percent of GNP (about three times the current level);

3. give assistance particularly to countries committed to meeting the basic needs and rights of their people;

4. put more emphasis on nutritional goals;

5. direct more research toward improving agriculture in the developing countries, whose climate, soils, and environmental conditions are very different from those in most developed countries, for whom most agricultural research currently is done;

6. increase U.S. support for multilateral institutions that have proven to be effective and that have the potential for being more effective in efforts to alleviate hunger and poverty.

7. improve the U.S. food aid program by giving food to countries on the basis of need rather than political ideology and in ways that reinforce self-reliant development.

Agriculture

Agriculture is the single most important business in the world. For a long time to come, it will also remain the largest business in the world. Multinational corporations can, and should be encouraged to, make a positive contribution in investment and research in the fight against hunger. The United States should:

1. encourage cooperation between developing countries and U.S. investors, especially small firms;

2. convene a meeting of corporate and agribusiness executives to discuss corporate assistance in the elimination of world hunger;

3. establish an emergency wheat reserve as a back-up to the Food Aid (P.L.) 480) program.

4. pursue a strong U.S. agricultural system by encouraging small- and medium-sized farms and by emphasizing conservation of soil and water resources.

This is an area where the United States has a particular role to play, both because of our traditional position as the world's bulwark against famine—a reputation of which we can be justly proud—and because of this is an area of undoubted American competence. Yet at the present time we are doing very little, in fact less and less in the way of technical assistance. We are putting about .17 percent of our GNP into development aid, in contrast to the U.N. recommendation of .7 percent. A number of other nations, with a lower gross national product, are doing much more. Ours is the lowest proportion of technical assistance of all the industrialized countries. This is a very grave portent for the future.

Conclusion

We are the country which invented the land-grant colleges. We are the country which invented agricultural extension. We are the country which invented rural credit with local banks financing local farmers. We are the only country in the world with sizeable grain reserves. And we also are the largest exporter of

71

food in the world, which gives us particular credibility. This is an area in which we ought to be working hard. It would be far better, and wiser, to win allies and work for world peace by leading the way in a development program to alleviate hunger and malnutrition than to count solely on an accumulation of atomic weapons to preserve peace in an increasingly chaotic world. That way can only lead to mutually assured destruction.

BOMBS AND BREAD

Gary Scott Smith

Reverend Gary Scott Smith is a professor of sociology at Grove City College in Pennsylvania. In the following statement, he explains the relationship between the arms race and world hunger.

Points to Consider

1. How much money is spent on the arms race?
2. What causes poverty and hunger?
3. How can military spending be reduced?
4. What specific actions can be taken to prevent hunger?

Gary Scott Smith, "Bombs and Bread", *Presbyterian Survey,* March, 1985, pp. 29–31.

President Eisenhower made the connection obvious: "Every gun that is made, every warship that is launched, every rocket fired signifies in the final sense a theft from those who hunger and are not fed, those who are cold and are not clothed." Let's stop this theft.

Our world suffers from two deplorable and increasingly desperate developments: an arms race that threatens to reduce our planet to rubble and the malnutrition and starvation that stalks one quarter of humanity. One problem cannot be solved without the other.

The world's resources are finite. While we spend trillions of dollars and use important non-renewable resources for defense, we do not have the money or the means to eliminate world hunger. And while we are expending so much time and energy on military research and development, on maintaining defense facilities around the world and on deploying more and more destructive weapons (or in arguing against these policies and seeking reductions of arms), we are unable to devote ourselves to removing malnutrition and starvation from our world. International tensions, produced in part by the arms race, compel developing nations as well to spend their limited funds on armaments rather than socioeconomic development. Moreover, Third World countries are not likely to enjoy political stability as long as millions of their people live in abject poverty and go to bed hungry every night.

The same forces operate to increase population and to constrain the food supply. The causes of poverty are complex, interrelated and many—depleted soils, unemployment, inflation, lack of education and skills, shortage of energy and technology, the absence of an infrastructure that can connect products with markets, the rich elite who exploit the masses, the oppressive system of tenant farming under which many of the poor live, and the policies of some multinational corporations.

The Two Wars

If the world's nations ceased all military spending tomorrow, it would not automatically solve the world's population and hunger problems. Other important steps would be necessary to channel time, energy and resources from battling political adver-

74

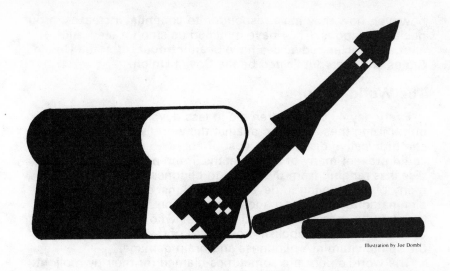

Illustration by Joe Dombi

saries to battling poverty. But consider how the two "wars" are related:

- Our world spends $600 billion a year on arms; spending for international development assistance is about $30 billion annually, only one-twentieth as much.
- The money our world spends in half a day on defense would be sufficient to finance the World Health Organization's entire program to combat malaria.
- For the cost of a single tank we could improve storage facilities for 100,000 tons of rice or provide classrooms for 30,000 children.
- For the price of a single jet fighter we could build 40,000 village pharmacies.
- With a mere 0.5 percent of the world's annual military expenditures we could buy enough farm equipment to enable most developing nations to supply their own food needs by 1990.
- About 40 percent of the world's scientists and engineers devote their talents and energies to military research.

Some say we cannot disarm or even reduce our military spending because of the Soviets. To do so would be absolute folly; it would make us vulnerable to a Soviet attack and might result in our subjugation by a wicked, totalitarian, atheistic regime.

We do not know how the Soviets would respond to a reduction in our armaments and military expenditures. We do know, however, how they have responded to continual increases of our nuclear weapons: They have matched us step for step. Almost all major nuclear advances have been introduced by the United States and then duplicated by the Soviet Union. . . .

The World's Poor

Every day 40,000 children die in less developed countries. By immunizing these children against the world's most common communicative diseases—a cost of about $5 per child—we could prevent many of these deaths. If the poor had pure water, diseases ranging from dysentery to blindness, which afflict many of those living in developing nations, could be largely eliminated. By providing adequate nutrition for the one-third of the children in less developed countries who do not have a decent diet, we could abolish most cases of dwarfism, curvature of the spine, vitamin A blindness and brain damage.

The world's poor are sometimes blamed for their own plight; they are called lazy, shiftless and immoral. These characteristics may describe some and malnutrition so debilitates others that they cannot work hard, but the vast majority labor long hours under difficult conditions. And given their land, resources and equipment, they are generally quite productive.

What usually prevents the indigent from having enough to eat is not his lack of ambition or his work habits but factors outside his control: droughts, floods, soaring inflation, landlords who charge interest rates of up to 50 percent a year, wars, the spending policies of his government, and lack of land, fertilizer, equipment and education.

The 1,500 scientists who participated in the National Academy of Sciences' thorough study of world hunger (1977) and the Presidential Commission on World Hunger (1980) agreed that the worst aspects of hunger and malnutrition can be eliminated within one generation if the human community acts cooperatively and decisively. World leaders from 22 nations declared in their joint statement at the Cancun Summit in October 1981 that "persistent and widespread manifestations of hunger are entirely incompatible with the level of development attained by the world economy and in particular the existing food production capacity." We have the technical and material resources to abolish hunger in our world; what we lack is the willingness to commit sufficient political and economic resources to this task.

Reducing Military Spending

What is required to abolish world hunger is the concerted actions of individuals, organizations and nations, and presently our preoccupation with the arms race impedes such a campaign. President Eisenhower made the connection obvious: "Every gun that is made, every warship that is launched, every rocket fired signifies in the final sense a theft from those who hunger and are not fed, those who are cold and are not clothed." Let's stop this theft.

What can we do as individuals and through local and national organizations to transfer our energies and finances from strengthening military defenses to aiding the hungry of the world?

- We can support measures that would shift tax dollars from military spending to economic aid that promotes self-development of poor peoples. By any reasonable standard, the United States has sufficient defensive capabilities. Together with the Soviets, we possess the ability to destroy the world many times over. Yet our government continues to plan to build even more terrifying weapons that will make our planet even more perilous. We might discover that if we change our priorities from military preparedness to helping less developed countries increase their productivity and standards of living, we could create stronger alliances and a more secure world.

- We can encourage members of Congress to support defense and developmental policies that rest on broader conceptions of global security and economic needs. Our present policies tend to be based upon our own interests and goals instead of those of the world.

- We can challenge our government to stop supporting repressive dictators and the wealthy elite in developing nations who do little or nothing to help the poor. During the past two decades much of our military and economic aid has gone to military regimes that permit no open opposition to the government and do not promote economic advancement for the masses. Aid to such countries tends to strengthen the power of the local elite whose control over land and other productive resources has helped to generate poverty and hunger.

- We can support Bread for the World. Pressure from this organization helped prompt Congress to mandate that 40 percent of our foreign aid be devoted to projects that directly benefit the "absolute poor" and to establish concrete standards that developing nations must meet in order to receive additional aid. . . .

- We can monitor the actions of transnational corporations we work for, buy from or own stock in to try to ensure that their policies have a positive rather than a negative impact upon Third World countries. The protests of sociologist Anthony Campolo and other stockholders prompted Gulf and Western to re-

Rethinking with Scripture

From Scripture there is much incentive to re-think the value of arms and allocations of resources. In the Old Testament the prophet Isaiah warns that the Lord disapproves of arming against one another because "he shall judge between the nations, and shall decide for many peoples. . . ." Instead, he exhorts, ". . . they shall beat their swords into plowshares and their spears into pruning hooks; nation shall not lift up sword against nation, neither shall they learn war any more." (Isaiah 2:4)

"Arms and World Hunger," *World Hunger Fact Sheet,* Church World Service, 1981.

evaluate its policies in the Dominican Republic and to spend $100 million to improve conditions there.

• We can give generously to church-related agencies that are directly involved in promoting self-development in the Third World. Because relief tends to destroy human dignity and to create dependence, we must move beyond relief to development assistance. Food aid often reinforces the structures in developing countries that cause hunger, frequently enriching the governing elite and allowing them to maintain low urban food prices that justify low industrial wages and discourage food production. Our goal should be to help the poor to develop skills and resources that will enable them to provide for their own needs. . . .

There are many obstacles to feeding the hungry of the world. Chief among them are the entrenched elite in developing nations who control both state and marketplace and frustrate many efforts to help their countries' poor people. There are structural barriers that stand in the way of assisting the malnourished, but our preoccupation with defense and our dedication of tremendous energy, time and resources to the arms race also prevent us from adequately addressing this problem.

Half of the world's people (living mostly in the Northern Hemisphere) consume 90 percent of its resources and spend billions of dollars to protect themselves from each other. The other half (living mostly in the Southern Hemisphere) use only 10 percent of the world's resources, and half of these people are malnourished, ill-clad and inadequately protected from the elements.

We can rationalize that our expenditures on defense are necessary to preserve our prosperous, democratic way of life and to enable us to continue to help the hungry in the significant but insufficient manner we presently do. But true security will not result from building more nuclear weapons. It will come from working to reduce tensions in our world by pursuing dialogue and negotiation with the Soviets and promoting economic and social development in the Third World.

God requires us to share our resources with those in need and to work diligently to create a world where all people have sufficient food, shelter and clothing. Let us shift our energies from an arms race to a race to end hunger, starvation and poverty.

MILITARY AID AND ECONOMIC SECURITY

Frank Wisner

Frank Wisner is the Deputy Assistant Secretary for African Affairs. He made the following statement before the Subcommittee on Africa of the House Foreign Affairs Committee.

Points to Consider

1. What percent of U.S. foreign assistance requests for Africa is in the form of economic and food aid?
2. Why is military aid necessary?
3. What military threats do African nations face?
4. Why is military assistance given to Mozambique?

Frank Wisner, "FY 1986 Assistance Requests for Sub-Sahara Africa", *Department of State Bulletin,* May, 1985, pp. 49–51.

By encouraging the development of an educated and professionalized military, our security assistance program reinforces the structure on which the stability necessary for economic growth and stability depend.

I am happy to discuss the Administration's foreign assistance proposals. I would like to concentrate my remarks on the overall policy setting—our goals and objectives in Africa and how the foreign assistance program fits into them. . . .

First, there has been the drought which has had such an immense tragic impact on many parts of Africa. We are proud that in the first 5 months of this fiscal year, we have committed $0.5 billion to supply a million tons of emergency food and other emergency supplies for 21 countries in Africa. . . .

However, it is not the drought which I wish to discuss with you today but rather the relationship of U.S. foreign assistance to Africa's long-term economic difficulties, what is often called "the African economic crisis." . . .

Whatever the causes, the results are clear. Africa is the only region in the world where per capita food production has declined over the past two decades and where dependency on imports continues to rise alarmingly (10 million tons of cereals per year at present). African GDPs [gross domestic products] continue to decline while debt soars. . . .

There is no American panacea for this situation. There is, however, an American plan for action. It is based on the recognition that Africa needs a variety of forms of assistance. In some cases—and there are various forms of this—food assistance may be appropriate while in other cases it would be harmful. In some cases balance-of-payments or budgetary support is crucial in order to maintain a multilateral pattern of assistance. In some cases such assistance would be useless since the recipient country is not prepared to undertake policies which will provide economic viability over the longer run. In virtually all cases we need to undertake longer term assistance programs—bilaterally, regionally, and multilaterally—to assist Africans to develop the human and physical infrastructure which will permit development over the coming decades. . . .

Security Assistance

Our security assistance program for Africa recognizes that political security and economic security are inextricably intertwined. It is concentrated in areas where we have security interests and where the threat is tangible and clear. We are painfully aware from the Soviet practice that massive arms aid tied to meager economic assistance results ultimately in structural disarmament—that is, the phenomena of "rusting-iron" monuments to military friendship found in areas where the local economy simply cannot support the maintenance of the military hardware provided. Almost 83% of our total foreign assistance request for Africa is in the form of economic and food aid. The relatively small military assistance request is almost all granted in recognition of Africa's massive economic problems. By encouraging the development of an educated and professionalized military, our security assistance program reinforces the structure on which the stability necessary for economic growth and stability depend.

We must recognize, however, that Africa faces genuine security threats. Our security assistance is intended to promote stability in the face of Libyan, Soviet, and Cuban adventurism. States threatened by this adventurism or hostile neighbors cannot devote the energy or resources necessary for economic development. U.S. assistance permits friendly countries to acquire modest quantities of military equipment in order to improve the border patrol and self-defense capabilities of their armed forces, thereby decreasing territorial threats and enhancing regional stability. Transfers of sophisticated weapons are discouraged.

Our request for FY 1986 is roughly the same as in FY 1985. Of our total 1986 request for Africa, just over $1.2 billion, only 17% is for military-related assistance. While the military component is small, it is, nevertheless, extremely important if we are to continue the programs of logistics and training that we have started and if we are to provide the bare minimum in the way of defense equipment for our friends facing threats.

In the Horn of Africa, our security assistance is directed toward:

● Helping Somalia defend itself against attacks by Ethiopian forces and Ethiopian-supported rebels;

● Assisting Sudan in protecting itself from Libyan incursions; and

● Helping Kenya and Djibouti to modernize their forces.

Defensive Efforts

These efforts are clearly—in magnitude and choice of equipment—defensive, not offensive. Our assistance is coupled with diplomatic efforts, by ourselves and our allies, to reduce tensions in the area and to find ways to diffuse tense border situations that could flare up into major military confrontations.

82

Military and Economic Aid

Members of Congress have examined our overseas programs. The Commission on Security and Economic Assistance, headed by Frank C. Carlucci, reviewed our total foreign assistance program. The National Bipartisan Commission on Central America, headed by Henry A. Kissinger, reviewed our national goals and needs for assistance in Central America. . . .

The Carlucci commission concluded: "The instrumentalities of foreign assistance are potent and essential tools that advance our interests. . . . On balance, it is the judgment of the Commission that U.S. assistance programs make an indispensable contribution to achieving foreign policy objectives."

Both commissions concluded that economic and military assistance are equally servants of our national interests. The Carlucci commission notes that rising standards of living in the Third World are vital to internal stability and external defense. Conversely, threats to stability impede development.

Secretary George Schultz before the House Foreign Affairs Committee, February 9, 1984.

Southern Africa remains an area of continued effort. Aid to nations in southern Africa (Botswana, Mozambique, and Zimbabwe) is geared toward reducing tensions and encouraging the evolution of an internationally acceptable agreement for the independence of Namibia.

Our initiative to provide security assistance to Mozambique warrants special mention. By providing nonlethal items—such as uniforms, communications equipment, trucks, and training—we are working in parallel with our allies to reinforce Mozambique's support of regional stability by offering an alternative to total dependence on the Eastern bloc for military supply. At the same time this assistance will bring the Mozambican Armed Forces into contact with the U.S. military.

A more detailed analysis of our request will put it in context. The 1986 MAP [military assistance program] request is for

$189.4 million; the 1985 request was for $190.5 million; and the actual allocation as a result of the continuing resolution process was $149.0 million. You can see that our 1986 request is virtually the same as the 1985 request. The 1986 FMS [foreign military sales] credit request is $18.0 million, up $8 million over 1985 as a result of an increase in Cameroon and the addition of $5.0 million for Gabon. Only three countries in sub-Saharan Africa receive FMS credits: Gabon, Cameroon, and Botswana. Our FY 1986 IMET [international military education and training] request is for $11.5 million. The FY 1985 request was for $11.1 million, and the actual allocation was $10.9 million. Our IMET program (request and actual) has remained remarkably constant and continues to be one of our most effective tools in Africa.

Three new programs are contained in the 1986 request. We propose a small MAP program for Equatorial Guinea. This $1.0 million program would begin to refurbish Equatorial Guinea's patrol boats and hopefully provide the navy with at least a minimal capability. The Soviets provided the original equipment and did not support it. The patrol craft are currently not in seaworthy condition. Equatorial Guinea is another of the growing list of countries that are turning to the West and the United States for assistance in the wake of Soviet mistreatment.

We also propose to begin small IMET programs in Sao Tome and in the Comoros. Both countries are well aware of the IMET program and are anxious to send a few officers to the United States for training. Relations have improved with both countries, and we would like to offer these programs as a demonstration of intention to continue the warming trend in our relationships as well as begin to have more contact with the military leadership which formerly had contacts only with the Soviet bloc.

FOREIGN ASSISTANCE TO
ETHIOPIA: AN OVERVIEW

R. Lynn Erickson

Relations between the United States and Ethiopia have shifted from close association until 1974 to the strain and hostility in recent years. The United States had been a long-time supporter of Emperor Haile Selassie's government in Ethiopia. With the expansion of Soviet influence in neighboring Somalia in the early 1970s, U.S. concern over the Soviet role in the strategic Horn of Africa, adjacent to the Red Sea and the Indian Ocean, increased. In addition to being criticized for his authoritarian and regressive rule, the Emperor was accused of being unresponsive to the worsening drought and severe famine facing Ethiopia and much of the rest of Africa in the early 1970s. Charges of "hiding" the famine from the international community and of insensitivity to the plight of his people contributed to Selassie's downfall. In 1974, Selassie was overthrown by Lt. Col. Mengitsu Haile Mariam, who established an avowedly Marxist-Leninist government and entered into a Treaty of Friendship and Cooperation with the Soviet Union. As many as 11,000 Cuban troops may be in the country today.

Currently, Mengitsu confronts many of the same problems that Selassie encountered. In addition to economic and development difficulties, the ongoing civil war waged by northern secessionists in Eritrea and Tigray, and continued tension with So-

R. Lynn Erickson, "U.S. Assistance to Ethiopia: Foreign Aid Facts", Library of Congress, December 27, 1984, pp. 2–5. R. Lynn Erickson is a foreign affairs specialist in the Library of Congress.

malia over the Ogaden region, Ethiopia is plagued by what has been called the worst drought of the century. . . .

In 1984 reports from Ethiopia's relief agency, the Relief and Rehabilitation Commission (RRC), estimated that 7.7 million people were affected by the drought, 5.5 million were threatened with starvation and 2.2 million have been forced from their homes. UNICEF officials estimated that 200 people were dying every day in Ethiopia's feeding camps. An expected food supply shortfall in December and January, in which thousands were expected to starve, has been averted by the diversion of ships to Ethiopia. . . .

Key Issues

(1) U.S.-Ethiopian political differences.

The Ethiopian government has frequently voiced anti-American sentiments while at the same time criticizing the United States for its refusal to make long-term investments in the country. Ethiopia has blamed the current hunger crisis on Western donor neglect, a charge which U.S. officials reject.

Facing difficulties in cooperating with Ethiopia following Mengitsu's takeover, the executive branch began to phase out the emergency food assistance program. In 1983, the Reagan Administration requested that the program for FY84 be eliminated in its entirety. This led to charges that the food aid program was being "politicized." Heightened awareness of the growing food crisis, in part resulting from congressional attention to the issue, led the Administration to restore Ethiopia's emergency food aid program.

Nonetheless, many continue to allege that the Administration responded only reluctantly to the famine. They note the case of a Catholic Relief Services request made in December 1982 that was not met until May 1983. U.S. officials assert that they responded to the Ethiopian famine as soon as reliable information on its scope became available. The United States supported international appeals for food relief in 1983 and 1984, they note, and AID Administrator M. Peter McPherson has called the recent U.S. response to the famine "enormous. . . ."

(2) Has Ethiopia's own response to the famine been adequate?

Some critics assert that the Ethiopian government is not adequately addressing the drought and famine. The Ethiopian government has been criticized for not giving food aid shipments priority, for example, and international relief agencies in Ethiopia have reported that prior to the country's 10th anniversary celebration, cases of cement and supplies from the Soviet Union were allowed to dock before a food shipment. . . .

86

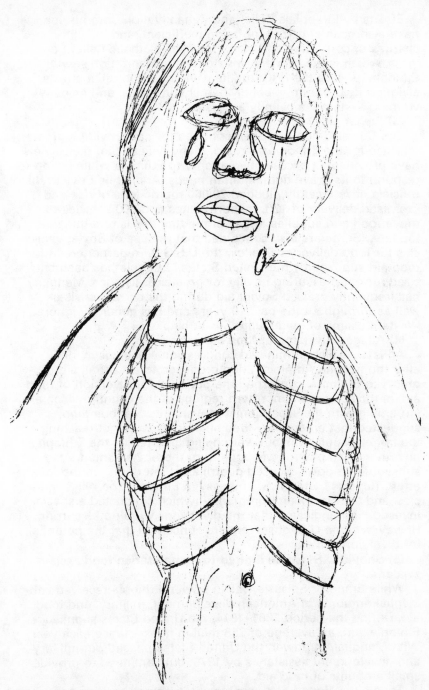

Marnie McCuen, age 8, March 1985, Hudson, Wisconsin.

Efforts by Ethiopia's Relief and Rehabilitation Commission have also been criticized for being inefficient, and in 1983 charges of corruption surfaced. However, Catholic Relief Services, which is the primary private relief organization serving Ethiopia, praises the RRC for "its well-organized relief efforts," claiming its program is better than any in Africa, and its early warning system "uncannily accurate. . . ."

(3) Soviet aid.

The Soviet Union has been criticized for not providing greater food aid for the Ethiopian famine. Many believe that the Soviets have provided an excess of weaponry to Ethiopia while failing to respond to its grave humanitarian needs. And while Soviet relief officials have recently pledged 20,000 metric tons of rice and promised delivery of 12 transport planes and 300 vehicles to move food and supplies, many argue that this is too little and too late. (Some are also concerned that the use of Soviet vehicles for food delivery will allow the U.S.S.R. to garner credit for food aid supplied by the United States.) Ethiopia has been criticized for not pressuring its ally for greater assistance. Mengitsu has frequently praised Soviet aid during the current crisis as well as throughout the past 10 years and has generally ignored Western claims of inadequate Soviet help.

(4) Alleged diversion of food aid.

An issue which dominated congressional debates in 1983, after the Reagan Administration proposed to cut off all aid programs to Ethiopia, concerned the potential for diversion of food aid, particularly in the northern regions of the country which are struggling with the secessionist movements. Various reports suggested that emergency food shipments were not reaching the target populations but were being diverted by the Ethiopian government to pay for weapons from the Soviet Union. Also, subsequent reports accused guerrillas of interfering in the relief effort. Reports by the U.S. Embassy in Ethiopia, the relief agencies, and the European Community (which conducted a special investigation) indicated that the diversions were not occurring. However, some U.S. observers are concerned that the potential for diversion still exists.

(5) Should U.S. aid be limited to humanitarian food assistance?

While Emperor Selassie was in power, Ethiopia received substantial amounts of American development, military, and food aid. During the period 1961–1974, the United States supplied Ethiopia with an average of $36 million in assistance each year. With Mengitsu in power, the United States phased out military and development assistance by 1979, but continued to provide small amounts of food aid.

Today, the United States is legally unable to provide economic assistance because the Ethiopian government has refused to compensate American firms and private individuals for property nationalized in the 1970s, following the change of government, and because the government is in arrears of more than one year on repayment of past U.S. foreign aid loans. Under the Hickenlooper Amendment to the Foreign Assistance Act of 1961 (section 620e, added in 1962), countries that do not satisfactorily settle such claims are ineligible for U.S. foreign assistance, except where the aid is for humanitarian purposes. (The President can waive this if "such a waiver is important to the national interests of the United States.") Pursuant to the Brooke Amendment, which has been attached annually to the Foreign Assistance Appropriations Act since 1976 (currently section 518), the United States cannot provide assistance to countries that are in default of aid loans for more than one year.

Given the gravity of the situation in Ethiopia and the dismal long-term agricultural outlook, some would like to see development assistance restored in an attempt to meet Ethiopia's long-term needs. Another view, however, is that U.S. development aid to Ethiopia would not be effective under the current economic environment in Ethiopia. Critics argue that the Marxist-oriented economy practiced by the Mengitsu government discourages peasant farmers from boosting their production. Establishing a U.S. development program in Ethiopia, they contend would waste scarce aid resources that could be effectively used in other famine-plagued countries in Africa. Currently, ongoing negotiations are taking place between the governments of the United States and Ethiopia in an attempt to settle the compensation claims, which are estimated to value $30 million.

HUNGER AND FOREIGN RELATIONS

ACHIEVEMENTS OF THE ETHIOPIAN REVOLUTION

Tesfatsion Medhanie

Tesfatsion Medhanie is an Eritrean. He has addressed the details and history of the Eritrean and Ethiopian problems in various socialist publications.

Points to Consider

1. What progress has been made during the Revolution?
2. How have the socialist nations helped Ethiopia?
3. What are the two major problems faced by Ethiopia?
4. What is the nature of U.S. policy in Eritrea?

Tesfatsion Medhanie, "The Ethiopian Revolution: Achievements, Problems and Prospects", **New World Review,** November–December, 1984, pp. 16–21.

The Reagan administration and its allies continue to try to exploit the famine situation even while they are sending food aid.

Despite the many internal and external difficulties the government and people of Ethiopia have faced during the first decade since the overthrow of Hailesellassie and the old feudal structure, they have made remarkable social and economic gains. The following are among the most significant.

Achievements of the Ethiopian Revolution

Agriculture and the peasantry: The first socio-economic problem addressed by the new regime was that of land and the peasantry. In March 1975 the Provisional Military Administrative Council (PMAC) took the most decisive and radical measure on this question. It nationalized all rural land, thereby terminating tenancy in the south and obsolete and cumbersome land tenure systems in the north. . . .

Industry and commerce: In early 1975 the PMAC nationalized major industrial firms, banks, and insurance companies. But it had allowed private enterprises to continue in some industrial and commercial activities.

The state sector in industry and commerce has been growing in the last decade. The PMAC nationalized more and more of the private enterprises. These include commercial farms raising coffee, sugar and cotton, many of which have now become "mechanized state farms."

At the beginning of the revolution the industrial sector contributed a small percentage of Ethiopia's gross national product. Today, as part of the state sector, it represents a significant proportion of the country's economy.

Literacy and education: Tremendous strides have been made in this area.

The new regime launched a vigorous literacy campaign. It assigned thousands of students to teach the alphabet throughout the country.

The campaign, conducted in the various national languages, has been going on for several years. It has been highly successful. It has raised the literacy rate from 7 per cent to over 60 per cent, and promises to raise it even more in the coming years.

The new government has also expanded the educational institutions. It has increased the number of secondary schools and the branches of the national university.

91

Health, infrastructure, and living conditions: Medical facilities have been expanded since the beginning of the revolution. A total of 86 hospitals, 1,200 outpatient clinics and 530 inoculation centers have been built. The number of Ethiopian medical personnel is said to have "multiplied many times."

Likewise, there have been improvements in the infrastructure of the country. Numerous roads and bridges have been built.

Efforts have been made to expedite the improvement in the life of the rural communities. For example, those who were sent to teach literacy also performed other tasks. They enlightened the rural peoples on hygiene, agriculture, and even on the harmfulness of certain gross traditional practices. They participated in projects involving actual physical work, as road construction and the digging of water wells. . . .

Food & Famine

In past years the West sought to use Ethiopia's food requirements as a weapon. The US administration and the British government in particular withheld food aid, unmistakably insisting Ethiopia should abandon its choice of the socialist path. . . .

Ultra right elements in the Reagan administration and in the media have, in various ways, indicated their intent to use the famine problem to campaign for the overthrow of the government and for the restoration of the capitalist road in Ethiopia. . . .

Several of them have declared the famine is the result of "socialism," contending socialism does not work. . . .

The case of Ethiopia demonstrates that the USSR and other socialist countries are the most dependable partners in the struggle of the young states for socio-economic development. They have provided Ethiopia with tremendous assistance in the industrial, agricultural, educational and cultural spheres—assistance which aims at solving the country's socio-economic problems in the most fundamental sense. In response to the present emergency:

• The USSR sent tons of food items. It provided over 300 trucks, a dozen airplanes and two dozen helicopters to carry supplies to famine victims in areas remote from the ports. It also provided a number of large water tank trucks, water drilling and pumping stations and specialists in this field.

• The German Democratic Republic allocated $8 million for immediate emergency aid to Ethiopia. It airlifted 3,000 tons of supplies including 200 tons of baby food, several tons of medicine, blankets and tents. It also sent 35 trucks.

• Bulgaria sent wheat and flour, trucks, tractors and water pumps.

• Hungary sent tons of various food products.

Source: FAO

- Poland delivered a large consignment of medicine.
- Czechoslovakia shipped a large volume of miscellaneous items.
- The People's Democratic Republic of Yemen (PDRY) sent 1,250 tons of wheat flour.
- Libya rushed a large team of doctors and nurses.

Ethiopia's leaders have expressed their gratitude to the peoples of the US and other donor countries for their positive response to the call for relief assistance. They have made it abundantly clear however that they resent all attempts to use the famine as an occasion for anti-socialist and other sinister designs. . . .

Soviet Assistance to Ethiopia

The following are some of the projects being carried out with Soviet assistance:

Industry and energy: The oil refinery at the port of Assab is the largest enterprise of the state sector. It operates efficiently and satisfies Ethiopia's requirements in basic kinds of oil products. The refinery was initially built by the USSR in 1961. In 1980 the USSR reconstructed the refinery greatly increasing its capacity, which has now reached 800,000 tons a year.

A thermal electric station was built at the refinery in Assab. This station has a capacity of 13.5 megavolts which satisfies the requirements of not only the factory but also the city and the port of Assab.

Preparations are underway for the construction of the country's largest hydroelectric station in the Melka-Wakana-Kaliti area. The station will have a capacity of 153 megavolts, with a transmission of 220 kilovolts.

The importance of the Melka-Wakana station to Ethiopia will be considerable. On its completion Ethiopia's capacity of electrical energy will be nearly doubled.

Mechanical engineering and metal work: A tractor assembly plant has been built in the town of Nazareth. It is designed to produce 1,000 tractors a year.

In August the enterprise produced the first tractors assembled in the country.

Several enterprises and plants are also being constructed for repair of automobiles, tractors and agricultural machines.

Construction and woodwork: Facilities are being set up for the production of construction materials, glass, lumber and other wood products.

A large cement factory is under construction in Dire-Dawa, with a production capacity of 600,000 tons a year.

Light industry and food industry: 18 granaries with an average capacity of 206,000 tons are being built. Six refrigeration plants with an average capacity of 4,100 tons are also under construction.

Material-technical base for modern agriculture: A struggle is being waged to achieve the material-technical base for increased agricultural production. The USSR has made provisions for the development of up to 110,000 hectares of land in the basins of the Baro-Akobo Rivers in the Gambela region. It has worked out complex schemes to develop the water and land reserves of this region.

The USSR is assisting Ethiopia in the fight against plant disease. It provided considerable assistance in the establishment of a phytopathological laboratory in the town of Ambo. . . .

Some Fundamental Problems

Revolutionary Ethiopia faces some fundamental problems requiring a careful approach. Most serious of these is that of nationalities.

Of all such questions that of Eritrea is the most grave and urgent. It is a problem which in origin predates the Ethiopian revolution.

Eritrea was colonized by the Italians in 1890. In 1941 fascist Italy lost the East African War and Eritrea was occupied by the British, who continued to "administer" it as a caretaker government.

In 1950 a US-dominated U.N. General Assembly resolved to join Eritrea in a "federation" with Hailesellassie's Ethiopia.

With the cooperation of the US, which in the early 1950s established military bases in Eritrea, Hailesellassie relentlessly violated Eritrea's autonomy and finally saw to the forcible dissolution of the "federation" in 1962. These violations spurred political struggles for independence which in turn led to the formation of an armed movement, the Eritrean Liberation Front (ELF).

The US had actively supported Hailesellasie's government in its efforts to suppress the Eritrean movement. But it changed its policy following the overthrow of Hailesellasie and the radicalization of the Ethiopian revolution along socialist lines. It gradually came to support the rightwing and sectarian factions in the Eritrean movement.

The strongest of these factions is the organization known as the Eritrean People's Liberation Front (EPLF). Emerging as a splinter group in 1970–71, the EPLF pursued divisive and destructive policies which polarized and weakened the Eritrean movement.

Ever since imperialism targeted revolutionary Ethiopia, the EPLF has become increasingly anti-Soviet. On the basis of that stance it established a most intimate alliance with a counterrevolutionary movement in Ethiopia's Tigrai province, known as the Tigrai People's Liberation Front (TPLF).

In 1980–81, the EPLF-TPLF alliance supported by the US, Iraq, Saudi Arabia, Sudan and other surrogates of Washington in the Middle East attacked the mainstream ELF, which was identified as the "pro-Soviet" force in Eritrea. They thus caused the end of its existence as an armed movement.

Food and U.S. Policy

US policy is now heavily manipulating the EPLF and other *armed* organizations in Eritrea. It is utilizing them to galvanize and sustain other "nationalist" movements in Ethiopia. These movements serve in the effort to destabilize Ethiopia and to combat socialist influence in the region.

In spite of this, the Eritrean question is still a genuine national question. It is a problem which calls for a political solution

Land Ownership and Famine

Usually soil erosion is linked to inequitable ownership of land. In countries like El Salvador, where in 1981 two per cent of the population owned 60 per cent of the land, small farmers have been forced to over-use their limited plots or to eke out a living from already marginal soil.

This is also one long-term cause of the famine in Ethiopia where, before the 1974 coup, the average landholding was just one hectare while thousands of square kilometres of arable land lay uncultivated by the big landlords. Peasants were forced to deforest and plant the hillsides, increasing erosion to the point where the highlands now lose one billion tons of topsoil each year.

New Internationalist, May, 1985.

within a framework which best guarantees unity between the anti-imperialist forces in Eritrea and Ethiopia.

Another serious problem facing Ethiopia today is that of drought and famine. This is actually a problem which has affected many other countries including 23 states in sub-Saharan Africa.

For the last several years neocolonial circles in the West have sought to exploit the problem to put pressure on the Ethiopian government. They have withheld food aid in the hope of forcing the government to abandon its choice of the socialist path.

The US and its Western allies are now donating food to Ethiopia. They have been prompted to do so by popular pressure and private humanitarian undertakings spurred in part by the wide publicity recently given the Ethiopian famine situation in the Western mass media.

But the Reagan administration and its allies continue to try to exploit the famine situation even while they are sending food aid. They are conducting a vicious propaganda campaign designed to villify Ethiopia's socialist orientation and turn the Ethiopian people against their government.

This propaganda falsely portrays the Ethiopian government as being insensitive to the plight of its people. It charges the government spent an exorbitant $150 to 200 million to celebrate the inauguration of the Workers' Party. It alleges that the government diverted food aid from the famine-stricken people to its armed forces engaged in campaigns against insurgencies.

The Administration also accuses the Ethiopian government of non-cooperation with relief agencies and donor governments. It charges that the state bureaucracy's sluggishness and excessive red tape weaken all aspects of relief operations in Ethiopia.

A number of relief workers and other observers have testified to the baselessness of these charges. They have praised the Ethiopian government's tremendous efforts to deal with this problem. They have noted that on the contrary, some Western governments—notably the Reagan administration and the Thatcher government in Britain—deliberately curtailed and delayed food aid, which they viewed as a weapon against Ethiopia.

A Prospect of Hope and Further Progress

Recent visitors to Ethiopia, including one of the two US journalists who reported on the inauguration of the Workers' Party, noted the "remarkable" changes which have taken place in the last decade. These changes show the viability of the socialist path and demonstrate the humaneness and effectiveness of socialist aid to the developing world.

Followers of Ethiopian events also note the gravity of some of the country's problems, including the Eritrean problem.

Socialism is capable of solving such problems as it has in the Soviet Union and other socialist countries. The growing commitment of Ethiopia to socialism would therefore raise the government's capacity and readiness to address and solve these problems in the best possible way.

There is reason to hope that for Ethiopia the coming decade will be one of speedier progress, unfettered by wars and famine.

ETHIOPIAN RULERS PROMOTE FAMINE AND WAR

Tigray Peoples Liberation Front and the Oromo Liberation Front

The Ethiopian government is engaged in an armed struggle with organized military units in the regions of Eritrea, Tigray, Oromia, Ogaden and Sidama. These groups are fighting for independence from Ethiopia. The Tigray and Oromo organizations present their case in the following statement.

Points to Consider

1. Why are famine and war the main features of the Dergue?
2. What is the main strategy of the military junta?
3. How is the resettlement policy described?
4. What actions can nations take to insure the delivery of food to starving people?

Reprinted from a joint statement by the Tigray Peoples Liberation Front and the Oromo Liberation Front, November 29, 1984.

Famine and war are the main features of the reign of the present junta.

Ten years after the previous famine that claimed the lives of close to a quarter of a million Ethiopians another one that may claim four times as many victims has gripped the attention of the world. Drought is almost universally blamed for the recurrence of a more widespread famine. Yet our peoples know that the unjust economic, political and military policies of the military junta—the Dergue—are more to blame for the present famine than just the vagaries of the weather. We believe that the urgency of reaching the victims of the famine should not hinder a sober diagnosis of the root causes of the problem. Failure to do this will result not only in inefficient relief work but also in prolonging and intensifying human suffering.

Famine and war are the main features of the reign of the present junta. After coming to power on the wave of popular indignation with the handling of the previous famine, staying in power became the junta's sole preoccupation. Hence, it diverted all resources to strengthen its security and military machinery at the expense of badly needed development projects to rectify the effects of famine and to avert its recurrence. On the contrary, it took steps that further deteriorated agricultural production throughout the country by perpetrating truly colossal destruction of human and material resources in order to perpetuate its widely detested dictatorial rule.

The re-emergence of drought not only exacerbated the situation but also served as a mute escape goat for the famine that is a cumulative outcome of its destructive acts throughout its ten year long rule. The fact that even areas that are normally producers of grain surplus, and that are not affected by the drought, are experiencing food scarcity is a glaring testimony to the fact that drought is not the only cause.

The Junta Strategy

Famine and the abuse of aid to starving communities figure prominently in the junta's strategy to cling to power. It normally destroys crops and cattle in its effort to subdue peoples that openly defy its dictatorial rule. After creating food shortages in this manner it appeals to the international community for food assistance with the primary intention of sustaining and expanding its large anti-people armed force—the main perpetrator of human and material destruction. This large armed force that is equipped with massive and sophisticated Soviet weaponry has proved ineffective in containing the popular struggles of the peoples of Eritrea, Tigray, Oromia, Ogaden, Sidama, etc. The growth of the national liberation movements and the emerging practical cooperation and solidarity between them have started to pose serious threats to its power. Now it plans to manipulate the famine to recoup what it lost in the political and military struggle.

The junta's plan to use relief assistance to entice people to areas outside their traditional habitat and into its garrison towns thus upsetting their economic and political activities, and screening them, is obvious to any observer. And the junta's practice of withholding relief aid from those whose loyalty to it is suspect has been widely reported. Such a callous handling of international generosity and employing famine as a political tool, we believe, deserves unqualified condemnation.

Resettlement Policy

The Dergue's proposed rehabilitation policy of launching massive resettlement of famine affected communities is also based mainly on political considerations. It is part of its strategy of pitting peoples against each other to prolong its fascist rule. The history of the Dergue's practice of resettlement has clearly proved that it only promotes alienation and conflict. In 1979–80 the military regime evacuated, very often forcibly, thousands of peasants from Wollo and Tigray and settled them in Oromia and other areas. These, who were ostensibly resettled for rehabilitation purposes, were forced to undergo military training and to be implicated in the junta's activity of suppressing legitimate national liberation movements of the Oromo and others. This wicked policy resulted in untold hardships for them and fostered enmity and friction between the settlers and the indigenous population. The Dergue is now scheming to intensify this policy by availing itself of the large number of helpless victims of famine and by tapping material and financial aid raised on their behalf.

The TPLF and OLF condemn this policy of denial of people's right to live in what is their ancestral homeland and settling them in that of others for political and military expediency. Massive evacuation of people who are in no position to make a deliberate choice about their future and manipulating it for political ends must be the object of an all round international condemnation.

Famine Victims

And all pressure must be brought to bear on the regime to allow relief supplies to reach famine victims wherever they are and without prejudice to their political affiliations. The effort to rehabilitate all affected communities should give priority to the

100

reclamation and effective utilization of the natural resources in their immediate vicinity and not such drastic measures as massive dislocation of population.

As saving lives ranks supreme in the priorities of our two fraternal organizations, the TPLF and OLF, we support the free movement of supplies and international relief workers in the whole of the famine stricken area. We call on all involved agencies to make special effort to reach our liberated areas where the majority of the people normally live.

We guarantee the security of the international relief workers and their supplies within the liberated areas and we are also ready to fully cooperate with all those who are trying to help millions of people who are on the brink of annihilation.

The TPLF and OLF fully support the formation of an international commission to supervise the fair distribution of food and other supplies, as we believe that it is the only sure way of eliminating partiality and discrimination on the basis of political affiliation and nationality.

Appreciating the quick response of the non-governmental, governments and the public at large gave to the plight of famine victims we appeal to them to see to it that all who need help benefit from their generosity.

As each passing day is claiming the lives of hundreds of children, women and men in the areas controlled by the liberation fronts we once again remind the international community at

Ethiopian Solution

Pressure appears to be building for massive aid from U.S. taxpayers to rescue the starving peasants of Ethiopia. President Reagan has already ordered hundreds of millions of dollars worth of emergency food aid. Congress will be considering additional millions worth. All this must of course come from the taxpayers.

Before committing ourselves to such expensive programs recognition should be made of the fact that previous U.S. aid programs have resulted in near total failure. Clearly a new approach in dispensing aid is called for. . . .

Because the famine in Ethiopia has been caused and made worse by the Communist government of that country, aid must be made contingent upon that government giving complete freedom to the various aid groups to dispense supplies wherever they are needed.

The Communist regime must not be permitted to use the aid program as a means to provide for its bureaucracy and armed forces while denying aid to the peasants in the distant regions of the country, some of which are in rebellion against the central government.

In any aid program in Ethiopia it should be made absolutely clear that any prospects for future aid will depend upon adoption of private enterprise and a free market with free prices in agriculture. To do otherwise would simply be acquiescence to continued support of a failing Socialism throughout Africa.

George S. Benson, *Looking Ahead,* April 7, 1985.

large that quick action is absolutely necessary. Finally, mindful of the anti-people record of the Ethiopian regime we call on all to be on the guard in any of their dealings with it.

INTERPRETING EDITORIAL CARTOONS

This activity may be used as an individualized study guide for students in libraries and resource centers or as a discussion catalyst in small group and classroom discussions.

Although cartoons are usually humorous, the main intent of most political cartoonists is not to entertain. Cartoons express serious social comment about important issues. Using graphic and visual arts, the cartoonist expresses opinions and attitudes. By employing an entertaining and often light-hearted visual format, cartoonists may have as much or more impact on national and world issues as editorial and syndicated columnists.

Points to Consider

1. Examine the cartoons in this activity.

ABCAP for *The People*/Socialist Labor Party.

2. How would you describe the message expressed in the ABCAP cartoon? In the Trever cartoon?

3. Do you agree with the messages in either of these cartoons? Why or why not?

4. Do either of the cartoons support the author's point of view in any of the readings in chapter three? If the answer is yes, be specific about which readings and why.

CHAPTER 4

A NEW INTERNATIONAL ECONOMIC ORDER: IDEAS IN CONFLICT

16

A NEW INTERNATIONAL ECONOMIC ORDER: IDEAS IN CONFLICT

JUSTICE BETWEEN NATIONS: PLANNING A NEW ECONOMIC ORDER

The Brandt Commission

The Brandt Commission report is the result of an independent investigation by a group of international statesmen, headed by Willy Brandt, into the urgent problems of inequality between the rich and poor nations. The report was titled, **North-South: A Program for Survival.**

Points to Consider

1. What is a real danger for the year 2000?
2. Why can mass poverty cause war?
3. Why is a new economic order needed?
4. What specific changes are recommended?

Willy Brandt, Chairman, *North-South: A Program for Survival*, MIT Press (Cambridge, MA: 1980), pp. 11–25 and 273–75. MIT paperback edition © 1980.

It is our conviction that we will have to face more seriously the need for a transfer of funds, especially in favour of the most handicapped developing countries.

Most people know that the existing system of international institutions was established at the end of the Second World War, thirty-five years ago, and that the South—mostly as latecomers on the international scene—faces numerous disadvantages which need fundamental correction. Hence the demand for a new international economic order. Fundamental change, of course, is not the result of paperwork but part of a historical process, of what is developing or foreshadowed in people's minds. . . .

There is a real danger that in the year 2000 a large part of the world's population will still be living in poverty. The world may become overpopulated and will certainly be overurbanized. Mass starvation and the dangers of destruction may be growing steadily—if a new major war has not already shaken the foundations of what we call world civilization. . . .

Our Report is based on what appears to be the simplest common interest: that mankind wants to survive, and one might even add has the moral obligation to survive. This not only raises the traditional questions of peace and war, but also of how to overcome world hunger, mass misery and alarming disparities between the living conditions of rich and poor. . . .

An End to Poverty and Hunger

It is a matter of humanity to conquer hunger and disease on our way to the next millennium—to prove wrong those forecasters who say we will have to face the distress of hundreds of millions of people suffering from starvation and preventable diseases at the turn of the twenty-first century. . . .

History has taught us that wars produce hunger, but we are less aware that mass poverty can lead to war or end in chaos. While hunger rules peace cannot prevail. He who wants to ban war must also ban mass poverty. Morally it makes no difference whether a human being is killed in war or is condemned to starve to death because of the indifference of others.

Mankind has never before had such ample technical and financial resources for coping with hunger and poverty. The immense task can be tackled once the necessary collective will is mobilized. What is necessary can be done, and must be done, in order to provide the conditions by which the poor can be saved from starvation as well as destructive confrontation. . . .

There will always be room for humanitarian aid, I believe, even in the most perfect social system imaginable—and, of course, even more so in a world with immense distress to overcome. But the international debate on development, at the threshold of the 1980s, deals not just with 'assistance' and 'aid' but with new structures. What is now on the agenda is a rearrangement of international relations, the building of a new order and a new kind of comprehensive approach to the problems of development.

Such a process of restructuring and renewal has to be guided by the principle of equal rights and opportunities: it should aim at fair compromise to overcome grave injustice, to reduce useless controversies, and to promote the interlocked welfare of nations. Experience has shown that much determination and purposeful effort will be required to produce structural changes with a fair balance and for mutual benefit.

A right to share in decision-making processes will be essential if the developing countries are to accept their proper share of responsibility for international political and economic affairs. It is this right which nourishes the aspirations of developing countries for a new international order, and these aspirations will have to materialize if relations are to be placed on a new basis of confidence and trust in international cooperation. . . .

Global Policies Needed

It is our conviction that we will have to face more seriously the need for a transfer of funds, especially in favour of the most handicapped developing countries, with a certain degree of automaticity and predictability disconnected from the uncertainties of national budgets and their underlying constraints. What is at stake are various possible forms of international levies.

Why should it be unrealistic to entertain the idea of imposing a suitable form of taxation on a sliding scale according to countries' ability? There could be even a small levy on international trade, or a heavier tax on arms exports. Additional revenues could be raised on the international commons, such as sea-bed minerals. While advancing such ideas, which are already under discussion in various circles, the Commission was aware of possible reservations. But—after an intensive exchange of views—we felt that new thinking is necessary to overcome the shortcomings of the present system of development assistance and at the same time strengthen the notion of universal, collective burden-sharing.

FOOD FOR THOUGHT

FARM BANKRUPTCIES

UNSOLD GRAIN WAREHOUSED

P.I.K.—GOV'T PAYS TO IDLE LAND

ETHIOPIA

Reprinted with permission of the *Minneapolis Star and Tribune.*

One might argue that it is hard to imagine international taxation without international government. But we believe that certain elements of what might be called international government are already called for to meet both mutual and national interests, and that by the end of this century the world will probably not be able to function without some practicable form of international taxation; and a decision-making process which goes a good deal beyond existing procedures. The survival of mankind, in justice and dignity, will make it necessary to use new methods to open new roads. But communications must be made widespread so that ordinary people know what is happening, and why.

None of the important problems between industrialized and developing countries can effectively be solved by confrontation: sensible solutions can only result from dialogue and cooperation. This demands a new perception of mutual dependence of states and people, to use the words of one of our colleagues. He added: development means interdependence, and both are preconditions of human survival.

There are many aspects of this interdependence: all nations will benefit from a strengthened global economy, reduced inflation and an improved climate for growth and investment. All nations will benefit from better management of the world's finite resources (and from a stabilization of the world's population). All nations—industrialized and developing, market or centrally planned economies—have a clear interest in greater security, and in improved political capability and leadership to manage global problems. But new vision will not end hard bargaining. . . .

International social justice should take into account the growing awareness of a fundamental equality and dignity among all men and women. Scientific, technological and economic opportunities should be developed to allow a more humane social and economic order for all people. Strong efforts should be made to further a growing recognition of human rights and of the rights of labour and international conventions for protecting them. . . .

A New Approach to Development Finance

The objectives we have defined above, together with others we discuss in our Report, will call for a transfer of funds on a very considerable scale. The dangers and hardships which will occur without it are unprecedented. There are pressing needs in food, in mineral and energy exploration and development— needs in the South whose satisfaction is important to the North. The plight of the poorest countries is desperate. A large range of other low-income developing countries need major support from concessional finance to accelerate growth and cope with balance of payments deficits. The middle-income countries have relied extensively on commercial borrowing, and measures are needed to ensure that they can continue to borrow from the market and manage their heavy debt burdens. Basing ourselves on the best available estimates made by a variety of agencies, we have concluded that the achievement of goals with which we could be satisfied will require sums equal to more than a doubling of the current $20 billion of annual official development assistance, together with substantial additional lending on market terms.

Such a substantial stepping-up of the financing of imports that are vital for world development would also serve to maintain and promote world trade on which the welfare of all countries depends. The economies of the North need to regain economic vitality but their intimate dependence on world markets makes it impossible for them to do this by trying to put their own house in order while forgetting about the rest of the world. Public and political leaders in all countries must be aware of the need to take determined action and to mobilize the political will. We envisage a new approach to development finance incorporating the following elements:

110

Exploiting Africa

Ever since capitalist Europe began to exploit Africa, the countries of that continent have been used as cheap sources of valuable materials, *including foodstuffs.*

Enormous crops of rice, coffee, tea and cotton were *taken out,* while the people were *forever hungry.* . . .

In the seventies Mali *shipped out* enormous crops of rice, 400 percent *more* cotton seed (oil), 70 percent *more* peanuts. While people starved.

And as for the "aid" sent to hungry Africa, from the West, it consisted mostly of *stale* (often spoiled) grain unsaleable on the world market.

The UNO surveys show that this "trade" (quality crops for sale in Western food markets, in return for "famine relief" supplies) costs Africans *$6,000,000,000 yearly!* . . .

As the FAO stresses, agricultural possibilities in Africa are *tremendous,* with excellent soils and climate. But the food today *leaves Africa,* to stuff the West's super-markets.

Northern Neighbors, February, 1985.

1. Funds for development must be recognized as a responsibility of the whole world community, and placed on a predictable and long-term basis. We believe all countries—West and East, and South, excepting the poorest countries—should contribute. Their contributions would be on a sliding scale related to national income, in what would amount to an element of universal taxation. There is an existing aid target for rich countries to provide 0.7 per cent of their gross national product as aid. For a country with average incomes of $6000, this would amount to $42 per person. The rich countries should commit themselves to a definite timetable for reaching the target, and for advancing towards one per cent before the year 2000.

2. We also believe more funds should be raised from 'automatic' sources. We have examined a number of possibilities including levies related to international trade, military expendi-

tures or arms exports, and revenues from the 'global commons', especially sea-bed minerals. Funds accruing from some of these new sources, insofar as they can be attributed to individual countries, would count towards aid targets. We believe that a system of universal and automatic contributions would help to establish the principle of global responsibility, and could be a step towards co-management of the world economy.

3. The World Bank and Regional Development Banks should take new steps to increase their lending. The World Bank is already doubling its capital to $80 billion. We urge that the statutes of the World Bank be amended to change its gearing ratio from 1 to 1 to 2 to 1 which would raise its borrowing capacity to $160 billion. With the record and prestige the Bank has built up, we believe that the change would not affect its market standing. We also call for a higher proportion of financing to be channelled through the Regional Development Banks, which should be similarly strengthened for this purpose. . . .

Power Sharing

While these specific tasks require major transfers of finance, we believe that the power and decision-making within monetary and financial institutions must also be shared more broadly, to give more responsibility to the developing world. This calls not only for the willingness of member governments to join in a revision of voting structures, but also for a style of management which exhibits closer understanding of and sensitivity to Third World problems, such as we put forward in our new institutional proposal.

A NEW INTERNATIONAL ECONOMIC ORDER: IDEAS IN CONFLICT

JUSTICE WITHIN NATIONS: THE REAL ECONOMIC PRIORITY

Bread for the World

Bread for the World is a non-profit religious organization that publishes information about the extent and causes of hunger and poverty in the world. Their address is 802 Rhode Island Avenue Northeast, Washington, D.C. 20018.

Points to Consider

1. What are two opposing ways of looking at world hunger and poverty?
2. What is the extent of landless people on a global scale?
3. What are the principal causes of poverty, hunger and injustice within poor nations?
4. What is meant by the "small farmer fallacy"?
5. Why could redistribution of land into small farms bring about impressive food production gains in the poor nations?

Bread for the World, *Land and Hunger: A Biblical Worldview,* 1982, pp. 11–21.

The widespread political movements that gained independence for most Third World countries generally did not address questions of domestic economic and social inequality.

Two common, but opposing, ways of looking at the existence of poverty and hunger in the world exist. One is fatalistic. It views hunger as a given. The impoverished suffer, but that is just the way things are in the world.

The other view is that the plight of the poor is not the consequence of a strange and uncontrollable phenomenon, but the result of a human-created disorder. Bread for the World members affirm the latter view. Life could be different if people behaved differently. . . .

Trends Toward Landlessness

Our review of land tenure patterns reveals the manner in which historical practices have created systems which gradually leave many people landless. Worldwide, the number of landless and near-landless people is growing fast. If current demographic and economic trends continue, one billion or more rural residents of the Third World will lack secure access to land by the turn of the century. Many of these people will migrate to the overflowing slums of the Third World cities. Some will appear as illegal aliens in the cities of richer countries. The malnutrition, illiteracy, poor health, and despair of those who stay behind will heighten tensions and instability in the countryside.

Rapid increase in landlessness is due in part to population growth. Other factors contributing include: ". . . the accumulation of land by better-off farmers; emergency sales of land by marginal owners; the spread of large commercial farms, sometimes foreign owned; and the eviction of tenants by landowners fearful of tenancy regulations or seeing a chance to profit from the use of new (seed) varieties and (agricultural) techniques."

Landlessness, and the poverty and hunger it produces, threatens the lives of millions of people. But that can be changed.

Power and Development

Unequal resource distribution, particularly with regard to land, has existed in all societies, and certainly predates colonial rule in the Third World. However, in most cases the colonial system intensified and reinforced existing inequalities. The widespread

114

political movements that gained independence for most Third World countries generally did not address questions of domestic economic and social inequality. Nor did they alter the fundamental power balance between rich and poor countries. . . .

Few of the benefits of development have reached the poorest groups. Many developing societies have experienced a further worsening of disparities in resource distribution. This is especially evident in the distribution of the most fertile farmland. Development efforts aimed primarily at promoting economic growth have usually resulted in even greater disparities between the powerful rich groups and the poor. . . .

The "Small Farmer" Fallacy

One of the principal reasons for the failure of programs to help the poorest has been the common and misleading use of the term "small farmers" to describe the rural poor. . . .

These owners of small farms are "seldom the majority of rural households and they are certainly not the poorest. Below them in status, influence and material welfare are landless workers, tenants and sharecroppers, and marginal farmers whose holdings are so small, often so fragmented and of such poor quality that they cannot provide a family livelihood from their holdings and must therefore deploy a large proportion of their family labor supply off the farm."

Development efforts directed towards farmers with small land holdings have often bypassed the poorest groups. In some cases they have even harmed them, for instance by promoting mechanization and reducing employment opportunities or by emphasizing production of non-food crops, which leads to a scarcity of food on the local market and consequently higher prices.

"People need assets—above all, land or assured employment at decent wages in order to benefit from economic growth. In many developing countries today, then, a 'basic needs' strategy must include reforms in land distribution and tenancy conditions if the lot of the intended beneficiaries is to be improved. . . ."

Land Use and Productivity

A common assumption is that larger farms are a more efficient way of producing higher yields per unit of land. It is assumed that farmers of large tracts of land can afford the latest technology—machines, new seed varieties, fertilizers, pesticides—and therefore can produce higher yields from the land than farmers of small family plots.

Is land redistribution to break up large farms thus likely to decrease agricultural production? The first factor to consider is that large farms tend to use less of their land to produce food. Much of it is left empty or grazed. . . .

Much evidence has been accumulated showing that small-scale farms can be highly productive. In fact, under similar ecological conditions, small farms tend to outproduce large farms, mainly because of the greater labor inputs and personal attention they are apt to receive.

A World Bank study, after investigating conditions in six countries—Brazil, Colombia, India, Malaysia, Pakistan and the Philippines—reached the following striking conclusion:

"Other factors remaining the same, a transition in each of these countries to uniformly small, family farms would increase national agricultural output by amounts ranging from 19 percent in India to 40 percent in Pakistan . . . In Brazil's northeastern region . . . the redistribution of land into small holdings there would cause an astounding 80 percent rise in the production."

Such research suggests that redistribution of the land into small farms could bring impressive production gains in developing countries which have too little land as well as in those where there is underutilization of the land. Farmers with small land holdings tend to cultivate their land much more intensively than those with large farms. They plant a greater part of it and, where climate permits, they also grow more crops per year. Huge farms are usually far less efficient in their use of land and capital than are small, family farms.

Productivity here is defined in terms of yield per acre. If productivity were measured as yield per unit of labor, large farms would have an advantage. But since most developing countries have an abundant supply of labor and a scarcity of land and capital, yield per acre is the most important consideration. . . .

Export Crop Production

Most Third World countries depend heavily on production of export crops to try to stimulate economic growth. What effect does increased export crop production have on the land and on the food supply?

In many Third World countries an increasing proportion of the best agricultural land is being converted to export crops such as sugar, bananas, pineapple, coffee, tea or rubber, in an attempt to increase foreign exchange earnings. In the Philippines the percentage of cropped land planted in export crops increased from 15 percent in 1960 to 30 percent in 1980. In Brazil, soybean production has increased fortyfold since 1966. In Nicaragua, land planted in cotton increased fourfold from 1952 to 1967, while grain acreage dropped by half.

Agony in Africa

But export crops do not just affect land allocation. Very often they claim the major share of agricultural credit; for instance, 90 percent of all agricultural credit granted in Colombia in 1965 went to coffee, cotton and sugar. Governments, eager to strengthen the export crop economy, and sensitive to the political influence of export crop producers, also frequently channel a disproportionate share of technical assistance to these crops, neglecting food producers.

Foreign-based companies grow crops in Third World countries in order to take advantage of cheap labor and raw materials and

117

Silent Emergency

The famine in Africa is but the tip of an iceberg—just one of the contributing factors to the overall world hunger problem that, by conservative estimates, leaves 450 million people chronically undernourished. . . .

For example, in a recent news conference largely ignored by the mainstream media UNICEF Executive Director James Grant pointed out that while one million children died from the famine in Africa last year, 15 million children die every year from lack of simple needs.

"The loud emergency—the Ethiopian famine—hits the news," said Grant, "but the silent emergency takes the great majority of these 15 million small children's lives each year. They are born to poor families in grossly underdeveloped situations, where mothers are illiterate, where there's no access to clean water, no health facilities. It's this which is the great killer."

The People, January 19, 1985.

---

thus maximize profits. An example of this trend is found in the Philippines. Del Monte Corporation in 1973 moved its pineapple plantations from Hawaii to the Philippines. The U.S. Congressional Record for November 9, 1973, states:

"While Hawaiian plantation workers earn $2.64 an hour, Del Monte pays its Philippine plantation workers 15 cents an hour. Hawaiian cannery workers get paid $2.69 an hour compared to the 20 cents an hour Del Monte pays Philippine workers for the same job."

Castle and Cooke (Dole) now owns 19,000 acres in the Philippines. Crops grown on this land are exported, principally to the United States and Japan, while malnutrition is a serious problem among Filipinos.

Similarly Mexico, during the winter, supplies over half of the U.S. supply of such vegetables as asparagus, cabbage, cantaloupe, cauliflower, cucumbers, strawberries and tomatoes. U.S. firms have shifted production from the United States to Mexico to exploit the wage differential. In the United States, firms paid asparagus growers 23 cents a pound for their crop. In Mexico growers receive 10 cents a pound.

As land is planted in export crops less land is available for local food production and total food output falls. This means that most Third World countries must rely on imported food which, unless subsidized in some manner, is more expensive. The people who have been displaced from the land and who cannot find adequate work, now face a reduced food supply.

Displacement

The growth of large farms using more machinery and less labor means that fewer people need to be employed in farm work. Small landowners who are bought out, tenants and sharecroppers who are no longer needed, are displaced from good land. They can leave the countryside to find work but the underdeveloped nature of most Third World economies means few employment opportunities for them. . . .

Responsible Stewardship

The problems of land use, export cropping and displacement of people provide us with vivid examples of the failure to follow ethical principles of land stewardship. It is a failure that must be addressed.

Land reform has the potential to promote fuller and more productive use of the earth's agricultural resources without abusing the land. This will require a willingness on the part of the powerful and affluent to share the earth's resources with those now dispossessed. That is a difficult task. But the ultimate benefits will accrue to all of humankind.

Effecting change will involve public and political, as well as private, action since present unjust conditions in the world are being perpetuated by human created disorders.

We can expand our world view to include the common good and future good of humankind. The challenge is to promote change leading to the ethical stewardship of the earth and its resources in all parts of the world.

A NEW INTERNATIONAL
ECONOMIC ORDER:
IDEAS IN CONFLICT

MAINTAINING JUSTICE IN THE PRESENT INTERNATIONAL ECONOMIC SYSTEM

Richard N. Cooper

The following comments by Richard N. Cooper were made in his capacity as Under Secretary of State for Economic Affairs. He cautions against any radical changes in the present global economic order.

Points to Consider

1. Why are developing countries important to the United States?
2. What demands are being made by the developing countries?
3. Why should the U.S. resist any radical changes in the present international economic order?
4. What kind of global economic system does the U.S. need?

Richard N. Cooper, "North-South Dialogue", U.S. Department of State Policy No. 182, May 15, 1980, pp. 2–3.

*We understand and sympathize with the
aspirations of the developing countries.
However, we also have an enormous stake in
the continuing smooth functioning of the
international economic system.*

For the United States, the developing countries are increasingly important both economically and politically. They are major suppliers of raw materials, including, of course, oil, and our most rapidly growing export markets. . . .

It is also in our strong security interest to see that most of these countries find that we and our allies are receptive to their desires for improved economic growth. It is true that so long as we maintain a strong national defense, the direct threat of developing countries to the physical security of the United States is negligible. But the internal upheavals and regional disputes can endanger individual Americans and risk confrontation between the superpowers. . . .

Perhaps even more important than these current considerations is the fact that the kind of world our children inherit will be heavily determined by the choices developing countries make as to their social and economic systems. The developing countries, after all, account for about three-quarters of the world population, and their share is increasing. The degree to which they identify or oppose the Western system of economic, social, and moral values will have an influence, perhaps even a determining influence, on whether our descendants live in a world which is hospitable to their values and welfare or whether they live under a psychological state of siege.

Developing Country Concerns

Thus, it is not only out of humanitarian concern but also for hardheaded economic and security reasons that the United States should listen carefully to the concerns enunciated by the developing countries in the North-South dialogue. These demands tend to revolve around three themes—obtaining needed foreign exchange, assuring availability of technology for development, and increasing the decisionmaking power of developing countries in the economic system.

The most important means of obtaining foreign exchange for most developing countries is through exporting raw materials or processed goods to the world community. Much of the North-South dialogue has therefore revolved around developing coun-

121

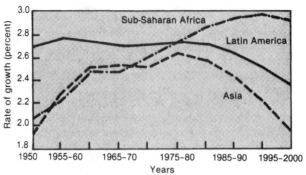

Source: Office of Technology Assessment.

tries' desire for higher and more stable prices for raw materials and improved market access for their manufactured goods.

Many developing countries, particularly the poorest, depend heavily on official development assistance to obtain their foreign exchange. They demand larger, more automatic transfers of resources on concessional terms with a minimum of political and economic strings attached.

Finally, developing countries, particularly the more advanced, can also open their doors to foreign investment or obtain loans from private capital markets. They obtain resources in the present in return for promising to allow payment of profit, interest, and principal in the future. The terms and conditions under which international investment and capital borrowing take place, and what happens when disputes arise, are therefore another important area of debate involving resource flows.

Developing countries also want to assure that increased resource flows will be used productively. To this end, they want to see increased the amount of scientific and technological research which will be of benefit to the developing world. They would like to improve the terms under which technology is transferred through private and public means to the developing world. Finally, they want to increase their own capacity to develop, select, adapt, and apply technology to their specific requirements. . . .

The developing countries have also sought through the North-South dialogue to increase their role in international economic decisionmaking. The dialogue itself, by highlighting the economic concerns of the developing countries, partly accomplishes this goal. In addition, the developing countries have pressed for increased voting power in institutions such as the IMF, have sought to move debate on particular issues to forums they find politically more hospitable (e.g., UNCTAD for trade), and have proposed new institutions in which they have a greater role at
122

the outset. The establishment of the International Fund for Agricultural Development, in which developing countries have two-thirds of the vote, and the voting structure being negotiated for a Common Fund, both reflect this pattern.

In sum, the goal of the developing countries in the North-South dialogue is to restructure the international economic system—to create a new international economic order—which has as primary objectives the promotion of their development and what they consider a more equitable distribution of the world's wealth.

U.S. Concerns

We understand and sympathize with the aspirations of the developing countries. However, we also have an enormous stake in the continuing smooth functioning of the international economic system. We are the world's largest exporter and importer of both raw materials and manufactured goods, the largest overseas investor, and the largest international debtor as well as the largest creditor. Major changes in the system can thus have important implications for our own welfare.

As we look back over the past three decades, we believe that the system has responded flexibly, if not always smoothly, to major changes in the world, including the growing economic and political importance of the developing countries. We favor continued evolution of the system to meet new situations. But suggested changes must have a high probability of improving the system for everyone—if this is not the case, it makes no sense to disrupt a system which works reasonably well.

We naturally have additional criteria with which we evaluate suggestions for changes in the system. We want a system which provides the stability and predictability that promotes trade and facilitates financial transactions—transactions which are increasingly long term in nature. This does not imply a system which resists change but rather recognizes that national social and economic structures can only absorb change at a reasonable pace. Sudden changes in the rules of the game for investment and financial transactions or massive shifts in trade patterns tend to inhibit overall economic activity. Thus, we favor needed change at a rate which can be absorbed without undue dislocations.

Second, we want an international system which promotes efficient use of the world's resources. As the current energy situation has made us painfully aware, we cannot afford to waste the world's resources—be they capital, raw materials, or human beings. We have thus pursued an international system of basically open trade and free capital flows. We are convinced that such a system will result in countries benefiting from their comparative advantage and increased global efficiency. . . .

Progress in Global Negotiations

In a sense, then, the North-South dialogue involves weighing a variety of politically, economically, and socially desirable goals—development, growth, efficiency, equity, and stability—in evaluating specific policy proposals. This is not dissimilar to the same kind of evaluation which the executive branch and the Congress must make in determining domestic policies. In both cases, it is a complicated process, but one in which progress is possible and imperative.

And progress has been made in the North-South dialogue. Measures have been taken which benefit both developed and developing countries and which have brought developing countries more fully into the international economic system.

A NEW INTERNATIONAL ECONOMIC ORDER: IDEAS IN CONFLICT

TRANSNATIONAL CORPORATIONS: PROFITTING IN HUMAN MISERY

José A. Benitez

José A. Benitez is a columnist for Granma, *the official newspaper of the Cuban Revolution.*

Points to Consider

1. How has the global status of hungry people changed in the last decade?
2. Why are the transnational corporations the major cause of hunger in Africa?
3. What role do Western banks play in the hunger problem?
4. How is the colonial legacy defined?

José A. Benitez, "The Imperialist Roots of Hunger", *Granma,* 1985.

The UN Commission on Transnational Corporations several years ago denounced the 156 transnationals controlling the world food sector.

Late in 1964—over 20 years ago—an FAO (UN Food and Agriculture Organization) report revealed that agricultural production in Latin America had grown less than 1 percent between 1961 and 1964, while the population there grew by over 5 percent. This only meant that more people went hungry in the region.

The situation has, of course, remained unchanged since that devastating FAO report was written; there are at present 130 million Latin Americans, out of a population of 400 million, suffering from malnutrition and 60 million are starving.

An FAO meeting was held in Rome last November and rendered another ugly report on the world food situation. One dramatic conclusion of the meeting was that during the past decade the number of starving people rose from 400 to 800 million.

Africa

This time Africa, with more than 150 million people on the brink of starvation, commanded special attention at the 86th FAO session.

"We are all agreed," said FAO Director-General Edouard Saouma, "that the current situation in Africa is truly tragic and, far from there being a possibility of noticeable improvement, everything would seem to indicate that the situation will worsen next year."

It is an objective fact that Africa is now afflicted with a prolonged drought that has millions of people in the African countries pretty near despair. All those people, the FAO has warned, are in urgent need of help and food.

Transnationals

But the drought is not at the root of the problem. The hunger afflicting the continent has its cause in the transnationals, the unequal trade under capitalism, the foreign debt, the transfer of know-how, the colonial legacy.

Africa is a continent rich in natural resources: hydrocarbons, uranium, gold, copper, phosphates, iron, diamonds, chromium, tungsten. It is a world exporter of cacao, coffee, cotton, peanuts, oil-producing seeds, sisal, sugar, tomato, olive oil, rubber. The

126

"I PLEDGE ALLEGIANCE TO THE FLAG OF THE COUNTRY THAT GIVES ME THE BEST DEAL ...."

MULTI-NATIONAL CORPORATIONS

"Paul Conrad, © 1975, Los Angeles Times. Reprinted with permission"

transnationals operating in Africa earn thousands of millions of dollars in profits annually.

But, far from reducing traditional agrarian inequalities, transnational agribusiness in Africa ensures that the best lands there end up in their hands.

With guaranteed financial backing, these transnationals are mainly concerned with the production of raw materials earmarked for export.

Transnationals are not new to African agriculture. Their presence in Africa dates back to early last century, engaged mainly in the exploitation of agricultural resources, and the supply of

Securing Privileges
for the Wealthy

The emphasis that governments of developing countries must choose their own development policies is undoubtedly sound. What is not so evident is that most governments do not have the luxury of working those policies out with full popular participation and support. Too often the inheritors of political or economic colonialisms who have entrenched privileges, often to the advantage of certain private sectors, are stoutly defended by U.S. corporations that themselves side with the privileged and use intense pressure on governments to perpetuate policies which at best are only marginally useful to society and at worst are a crass protection of the wealthy against the poor. For corporations to be credible as participants in the war on hunger they must, at the very least, refrain from using their influence or economic activity to pressure governments to secure privileges for the wealthy few to the detriment of the many who are hungry and poor. Just as this report calls for our government to move in a whole new direction on behalf of the hungry of the world, I believe the report also calls for a major redirection in the activity of U.S. multinational corporations to support social policies that benefit the many and not just the privileged few.

Eugene L. Stockwell, *Report of the Presidential Commission on World Hunger,* March, 1980.

agricultural produce and livestock to the industrialized capitalist countries.

The UN Commission on Transnational Corporations several years ago denounced the 156 transnationals controlling the world food sector. Close to 90 of these transnationals were U.S.-owned and their annual profits exceeded $100,000 million.

Unequal trade relations with the industrially developed capitalist countries and the public debt are two other factors that are to blame for the African food crisis.

In 1983, the Western banks received from the Third World roughly $70,000 million in foreign debt service charges. This debt now stands at $800,000 million. A part of the above service charges came from Africa, whose foreign debt is tagged at $150,000 million. This means that, while millions of Africans are starving, thousands of millions of dollars are pocketed by the transnational banks.

The world price of many raw materials exported by Africa experienced a substantial drop last June. A ton of copper, for example, could purchase roughly 115 barrels of oil in 1975, while now it can hardly buy 40. In 1960, a ton of coffee could buy 37 tons of fertilizer, but nowadays it is enough for only 15. In 1975, a ton of cotton was equal to 119 barrels of oil, but now it is equal to only 35.

Paradoxically, Africa has the world's largest water reserves. The water contained in the great rivers and lakes could irrigate the lands afflicted by drought, mitigate the evil of hunger, make the desert recede. Yet, what few irrigation facilities now exist in Africa are used solely to raise export crops.

There are endless possibilities in times like ours when scientific and technical progress has become a fundamental factor in agricultural production.

Colonial Legacy

The colonialists' legacy is patently visible in the drought and starvation afflicting Africa, in the illiteracy, economic and financial dependency, backwardness, neo-colonial structures, production mechanisms, weak economy and lack of qualified workers.

The social effects of such a legacy are disturbing: backward agriculture based on obsolete methods, and infant mortality rate of 200 for every 1,000 live births, the impoverishment of the small peasants, the exodus to the cities, the reduced nutritional value of food.

The colonial apparatus inherited by the liberated countries cannot, of course, be immediately restructured and can only be uprooted with flexibility and the transformation of the relations of production.

In the specific case of Ethiopia, as pinpointed in the last devastating FAO report, the eradication of poverty, starvation and the differences between city and countryside, and the establishment of external economic relations on entirely new basis form part of a long and complex process.

Hunger is not inevitable. As was once said—and must be borne very much in mind—wherever it rears its ugly head there are identifiable forces that can be checked.

20

A NEW INTERNATIONAL ECONOMIC ORDER: IDEAS IN CONFLICT

THE MULTINATIONALS' ROLE IN HELPING POOR NATIONS

Presidential Commission on World Hunger

The following comments are reprinted from the report of the Presidential Commission on World Hunger titled **Overcoming World Hunger: The Challenge Ahead** *issued in March of 1980.*

Points to Consider

1. What are some of the most important hunger reducing investments in developing nations?
2. What is the extent of corporate investment in developing countries?
3. What are the most appropriate roles for multinational corporations to play in Third World food systems?
4. What are the most inappropriate roles?

Overcoming World Hunger: The Challenge Ahead, Report of the Presidential Commission on World Hunger, March, 1980, pp. 75–79.

Past experience indicates that the U.S. private sector can perform a number of important functions that can aid the modernization of food systems in developing countries.

American involvement with food systems abroad has encompassed a wide spectrum of activities in both the public and private sectors. Out of the successes and failures that have occurred, has come a better understanding of the benefits and limitations of each. Perhaps the most important conclusions are that each group has a valuable role to play; that the issue is not generally public *versus* private, but the right combination of each under the right conditions; and that the conditions that are "right" vary enormously from country to country, depending on the respective stage of development, development priorities established by the country, and the services offered by prospective foreign investors.

The Potential

In assessing the potential of private U.S. investment to help alleviate world hunger, the Commission has focused largely upon the activities of agribusiness firms. For the most part, such activities involve the direct production of plant and animal products. Investment patterns in this area have undergone far-reaching changes over time. Large foreign-owned plantations have long since given way to modes of investment which do not involve direct ownership of land. Today, U.S. firms concentrate increasingly on providing the specific processing technology to expand the market and infrastructure for nearby small-holder growers.

A second important area of agribusiness investment involves the sale of goods (such as food products and agricultural inputs that include seeds, fertilizer, and pesticides) produced outside the host country, often by the parent company. The third major type of agribusiness investment concerns the processing of locally-grown agricultural products for export to developed countries.

Finally, some of the most important hunger-reducing investments in less developed countries—the construction of rural roads, irrigation and drainage systems, for example—require the planning and engineering talent contained within large private construction firms, many of them U.S.-owned. Although such enterprises are frequently forgotten in discussions of world hun-

131

ger, these firms are a dominant form of U.S. private activity in the developing world.

Corporate Investment

While the activities of agribusiness and construction firms together constitute less than one-third of all U.S. corporate investment in the developing world, total corporate investment in developing nations has grown rapidly in recent years. Between 1967–1976 the total grew from $33 billion to $67 billion—although it is important to note that over half that amount is concentrated in twelve countries, such as South Korea, Mexico and Brazil, with per capita incomes of over $1,000 per year. By 1977, the developing nations were host to more than 20,000 affiliates of international corporations, of which about half were American.

Corporate investment, then, has far-reaching implications for efforts to alleviate world hunger—both through direct involvement in national food systems and, more generally, through its impacts upon employment levels, purchasing power, income distribution, balance of payments questions and productivity in developing nations. . . .

Appropriate Roles

There is broad consensus among business and non-business analysts, from the developing as well as the developed countries, concerning the positive roles that multinational corporations in the food and agriculture sector can play in Third World food systems. The most important contributions are access to large amounts of international capital and credit, and established access to restricted international markets. Increasingly, multinationals act as marketing channels between the resources of the developing world, and the demands of the developed world. These corporations can also provide access to technology, scientific expertise and extensive research capabilities, combined with the managerial skills needed to translate laboratory findings into viable market operations. Additional advantages that such firms have include the economic strength to take substantial risks, and the ability to work with governments of different political orientations.

The special capabilities of agribusiness corporations are most likely to be maximized through investments in specific areas of interest to developing nation governments seeking to modernize their food systems. For example, through investments in facilities and services to conserve food and prevent food loss, such as rural storage and drying facilities, foreign firms can play a role in reducing post-harvest losses. The development of "in-

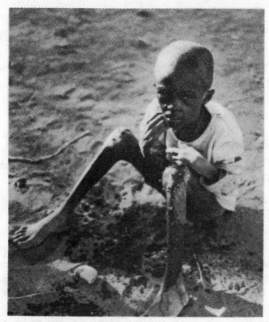

Source: Horizons, 1984.

country" food processing facilities can help to save foreign exchange on items that would otherwise have to be imported, and to earn foreign exchange by adding value to locally produced items for export.

In addition, the establishment of food fortification facilities, either at central locations or small rural mills, can upgrade the nutritional levels of traditional foods. Suppliers of farm inputs can help to increase crop and animal yields, and thereby expand the availability of food for local consumption and/or export. Marketing services and facilities to promote exports can then complement the direct production of commodities for export. Agribusiness firms can also provide on-the-job training for such tasks as the use of fertilizers, agrochemicals and farm equipment. Finally, in cases where equity investment is not desirable, corporations can provide appropriate skills, training and expertise in all of the areas noted above through the use of management contracts or other innovative arrangements.

There are also a number of investment options for which agribusiness multinationals are at a comparative disadvantage. The first is the direct production of staple crops. For the major field crops used for human food—wheat, corn, sorghum, rice, soybeans and other oilseed crops—direct corporate ownership of farming units has not become widespread even in developed countries. The family farm unit—whether large or small—combining ownership and management continues to remain the most productive, efficient unit. This is even more the case in poor countries, where it is difficult to assemble large land units, where governments generally oppose foreign ownership of land, and where major disincentives such as inadequate access to credit and water often work against increases in output even by local farmers.

Inappropriate Roles

The second type of investment option which is generally considered inappropriate for foreign corporations concerns the internal distribution and marketing of basic foods. A primary talent that American corporations have to offer lies in increasing the availability of a wide variety of foods in situations where the actual or potential market is large enough to justify the investment. However, transferring that talent to diverse developing country situations is a major challenge to American enterprise. Most large U.S. corporations have little experience and expertise when it comes to marketing basic foods to low income, widely dispersed consumers in the poorest countries.

On the contrary, agribusiness firms tend to produce "luxury" items for export or local consumption by the affluent. The poor majority in developing nations do not yet have the purchasing power to afford beef, chicken, strawberries or highly processed foods. To the extent that the production of such items diverts local resources away from the production of basic food crops for the underfed population, the effect can be negative in terms of alleviating hunger and poverty. . . .

Serious problems have also resulted when foreign firms have sought to expand their sales of these same products among poor people who can ill afford such goods, in either financial or nutritional terms. Often, sales are promoted through the use of

134

highly sophisticated advertising and other marketing techniques. The sale of food and drink of questionable dietary value, often a highly profitable practice, frequently contributes to poor dietary practices and lower nutritional levels among the poor, especially when scarce household income is diverted to buy such products. One example of this risk has been the marketing of infant formula to poor women in developing countries, as an expensive and potentially dangerous alternative to breast feeding in the absence of proper conditions for preparing and using these products.

Conclusion

In summary, past experience indicates that the U.S. private sector can perform a number of important functions that can aid the modernization of food systems in developing countries. On the other hand, the record also shows that some corporations have engaged in practices and patterns of investment which undercut or conflict with efforts to alleviate hunger and malnutrition in developing countries. Given the diverse food requirements, farming systems, natural resources and forms of government within the developing world, the nature and extent of mutually beneficial investment opportunities is likely to vary from country to country.

Generally speaking, however, the most attractive countries for foreign investors remain the middle- and upper-income developing countries where rapid advances are being made in industrialization and the expansion of economic and social infrastructure. In the poorer developing countries, which also are those with the greatest food problems, the critical lack of trained manpower and the need for infrastructure, such as farm-to-market roads, irrigation systems, and newer port facilities, offer little incentive to foreign corporations to begin operations.

More specifically, neither corporations nor developing countries see much of a role for foreign private investment in direct efforts to alleviate hunger and malnutrition among the very poor. Agribusiness executives themselves are virtually unanimous in recognizing the limitations of their own organizations for meeting these particular needs. They generally conclude that it is extremely difficult for a private business to develop, distribute and sell enough basic foods to realize even modest profits. Nor have most U.S. corporations applied their research and development efforts to the needs of malnourished populations. Food processors, traditionally, have target groups other than the poor. The techniques in which they excel—product differentiation, mass marketing to middle- and upper-income groups—historically have not met the needs of malnourished people in very poor countries.

A NEW INTERNATIONAL
ECONOMIC ORDER:
IDEAS IN CONFLICT

RICH NATIONS, POOR NATIONS: THE POINT

Ernest Harsch

Ernest Harsch is the managing editor of Intercontinental Press *magazine, which specializes in analysis of socialist, colonial independence, black and women's liberation movements and other global political events.*

Points to Consider

1. Who do Western nations blame for the African famine?
2. What is the legacy of colonialism?
3. What is the relationship between capitalist countries and the economies of poor African nations?
4. What is the cure for poverty and hunger in African nations?

Ernest Harsch, "Famine: A Fruit of Imperialist Oppression", *Intercontinental Press*, February 18, 1985, pp. 82–85.

Before the advent of colonialism, most African communities were largely self-sufficient in food production.

For the past two years, famine has been spreading across the continent. Ethiopia, which is particularly hard hit, has recently received some international publicity. But Ethiopia is far from alone. Drought and famine have already touched some 36 African countries. And in the rest, hunger and misery remain a constant feature of life for the masses of the oppressed and exploited. . . .

According to the Western nations, it is nature that is to blame—or the African peoples themselves.

In the United States, and Western Europe, the big-business news media, government figures, and officials of various relief agencies have often pointed to the severe drought that has plagued Africa over the past few years as the cause of the famine.

But this ignores the fact that droughts, floods, blights, and other natural disasters strike the United States and other Western countries from time to time without causing famine. Food and water storage facilities, efficient irrigation, and a highly developed transportation system help prevent such natural disasters from turning into human tragedies.

Adequate economic development can also overcome some chronic natural limitations. Southern California, for example, has a very low annual rainfall, and its aridity equals that of some deserts. Yet with the aid of widespread irrigation, it has been transformed into one of the most fertile farming areas in the United States. . . .

Legacy of Colonialism

Before the advent of colonialism, most African communities were largely self-sufficient in food production, though they were also generally poor. Despite their low level of technology, in many areas African peoples practiced irrigation, crop rotation, terracing, manuring, and the use of mixed crops to enhance soil fertility. They were careful not to overfarm or overgraze Africa's often fragile soil.

But in the 16th century, the colonial slave trade began. Millions of Africans were torn from their land and homes and shipped to the European colonies in the Western hemisphere, many dying along the way. African societies were undermined, and entire areas were largely depopulated. Communities were

137

frequently deprived of their most productive members, and agricultural production suffered as a consequence. In some areas, because of the loss of the bulk of all young males, women were compelled to perform almost all agricultural labor (a pattern that persists in a number of African countries today).

In addition, cheap European goods flooded into Africa in payment for the slaves, undermining indigenous textile, metalware, and other trades, and thus further weakening the local economies.

Following the abolition of the slave trade in the 19th century, the emerging imperialist powers of Europe continued to expand their markets in Africa. While developing extractive mining industries, they also transformed the nature of agricultural production in many regions by imposing the production of cash crops. These crops were destined for export to Europe and North America, to service those countries' domestic needs.

Colonial settlers and trading companies seized millions of acres of the best land for cotton, rubber, palm oil, coffee, tea, sugar, and other plantations.

African peasants were likewise compelled—through armed force, compulsory taxes, and the pressures of the market—to shift from food cultivation to the production of such cash crops. Since they no longer grew their own food, they had to buy it from elsewhere, with the earnings from the sale of their export crops. The most productive sectors of the African peasantry thus became tied into the world capitalist market—and made dependent on it.

While the European colonial powers finally relinquished their direct political rule over Africa and turned the reins of government over to African neocolonial regimes, the economic relations established under colonialism remained largely intact.

Capitalist market and production relations continued to develop in Africa. The continent's economies became increasingly dependent on the imperialist powers and ever more vulnerable to the fluctuations of the world capitalist market.

This is especially true for those countries where only one or two cash crops account for most of their export earnings. In Ethiopia, for example, coffee comprises 69% of the value of all exports, while in Burundi it is 93% and Rwanda, 71%. Cotton accounts for 80% of the export earnings of Chad and 65% of the Sudan's. For Ghana, cocoa accounts for 61% and for Equatorial Guinea, 66% (with coffee taking another 24%). In Gambia and Guinea-Bissau, groundnuts (peanuts) make up 90% and 60% respectively. Some 68% of Mauritius' export earnings come from sugar, as do 54% of Swaziland's.

Not only do the prices these countries receive for their export crops fluctuate wildly, but they are low in comparison to the

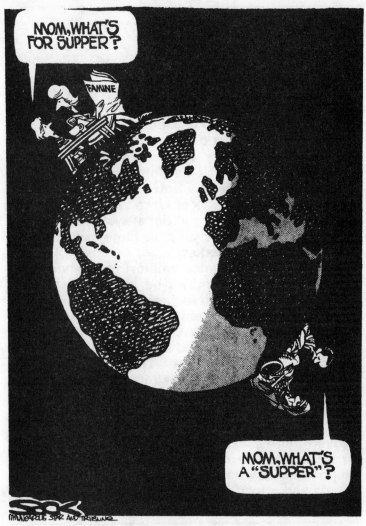

Reprinted with permission from the *Minneapolis Star and Tribune*.

costs of imported manufactured goods and oil. And the terms of trade are turning increasingly to their disadvantage.

With the exception of South Africa, where the extreme oppression and exploitation of the Black majority has made possible a significant degree of capitalist industrialization, the continent remains largely poor and underdeveloped.

This is particularly true in the countryside. Most peasants remain engaged in subsistence—or below-subsistence—agriculture, using the most primitive tools and with few resources or

139

Man-Made Famine

The African famine is largely man-made, the hideous result of capitalist priorities.

It has taken only a short time, as continents go, to destroy Africa's self-sufficiency in food, reduce fertile areas to wasteland and millions of its people to starvation.

Exactly 100 years ago the major European powers met at the Berlin Conference to divide among themselves the entire continent. They stepped up their plunder of Africa's mineral wealth and the disruption of traditional systems of producing food to make way for huge cash crops for the European market.

In the 30 years since political independence for most African countries began, the Western powers have reasserted their economic domination over the continent. The neocolonialists of Western Europe and the U.S. have poured in billions of dollars to be used almost exclusively on Western-approved projects. The projects rarely include agricultural production for home consumption, often siphon material and labor away from farming and usually increase dependence on the foreign "donors." Progressive African governments, attempting to avoid entanglement in the neocolonial net, have been handicapped in fostering food production by lack of funds and armed invasions.

Guardian, November 28, 1984.

social amenities. According to the United Nations' Food and Agricultural Organization, just 1.9 percent of Africa's arable land was under irrigation as of 1980. Hand tools were by far the main farming implements. Tractors and machinery (used overwhelmingly in the cash-crop sector) are involved in only 2 percent of all agricultural labor, and draught animals in just 13 percent. Back-breaking human labor makes up the remaining 85 percent.

Under such conditions, it is not surprising that agricultural production has stagnated. And with the steady rise in population, this has actually meant a *decline* in food production in relation to the continent's real needs.

Sub-Saharan Africa is the only region of the world where per capita food production has fallen over the past two decades. In 1980, it was 15 percent below the level of the early 1970s and 20 percent below that of the early 1960s.

As a result, more and more food had to be bought from abroad. Over the past 10 years, the amount of food imported by African countries has nearly tripled. Reflecting the rising costs of such imports, however, they have had to pay five times as much for them. But with the disastrous impact on Africa of the world capitalist economic recession since the early 1970s, they have had even fewer funds with which to purchase food to feed their hungry populations.

The prices these countries receive for the exported minerals and cash crops have fallen even further, while their foreign debts have skyrocketed. Between 1970 and 1982, sub-Saharan Africa's foreign debts increased by nearly 10 times, from $5.7 billion to $51.3 billion. By 1984, the interest and other debt servicing payments had climbed to some $10 billion a year. This has eaten up more than a quarter of these countries' already meager export earnings.

In this context, the onset of the most recent drought was a burden that Africa's weakest economies simply could not bear. Hundreds of thousands who were already living at the brink of starvation were pushed over the edge.

The Western nations, of course, have sought to cover up the real reasons for this famine. . . .

The Limits of 'Aid'

The African countries that are now affected by drought and famine need prompt shipments of international food aid if millions are to be saved from starvation in the coming months. So far, they have not gotten anything close to what they need.

The Western powers—whose centuries-long plunder and domination of the continent has set the stage for the famine—bear the greatest responsibility for providing this food aid. The U.S. government alone could easily purchase the necessary amount of grain from U.S. farmers, at fair prices, and distribute it free to all those who need it. With the $2.5 billion it spent last year on the MX missile alone, for example, it would have been possible to finance the total amount of African wheat imports in 1979.

Such aid, moreover, must be provided without any political strings attached. That is not the case today. Not only do the Western powers give only a small fraction of what is needed and what they are capable of giving, but they use the current food relief programs as political weapons. They often withhold it from those governments that defy their dictates, and provide it to those regimes that bow before Washington and the former colonial powers. They use it to pressure and blackmail. . . .

In President Reagan's January 3 address, he proposed the launching of a "Food for Progress" program under which food aid would be funneled to those countries where agriculture is based on "market principles" and "private sector involvement"—that is, cut-throat capitalism.

Within the recipient countries themselves, this kind of international aid does very little to benefit the poorest and most exploited sectors of the population.

Given the corrupt and neocolonial character of most African governments, large amounts of food aid never reach those who need it the most. It is hoarded, smuggled to other countries, or diverted to the "free" market, at prices that most people cannot afford and where profiteers can greatly enrich themselves. . . .

'The Cure Must Be Political'

Speaking for a country that has itself been the object of various "aid" programs, Burkina's President Thomas Sankara declared in a speech before the United Nations General Assembly on Oct. 4, 1984, "It is easy to see why the indignation of the peoples is easily transformed into rebellion and revolution in the face of the crumbs tossed to them in the ignominious form of some aid, to which utterly humiliating conditions are sometimes attached." . . .

After noting the legacy of poverty, disease, and illiteracy left to his country by a century of French colonial domination, Sankara pointed to the heart of the problem. "The source of the evil was political," he said, "and so the only cure must be a political one."

As long as the underlying social and political conditions that have bred the current famine exist, Africa will be plagued by hunger and starvation. Millions more will die, victims of capitalist greed.

The sole effective program to combat famine is to struggle against Western oppression. That is the root of the continent's misery.

A NEW INTERNATIONAL ECONOMIC ORDER: IDEAS IN CONFLICT

RICH NATIONS, POOR NATIONS: THE COUNTERPOINT

Lay Commission on Catholic Social Teaching and the U.S. Economy

In January 1984, in a wide-ranging conversation in New York, George J. Gillespie, Michael Joyce and William E. Simon, former Secretary of the Treasury, came up with an idea: Why not form a committee of lay Catholics to respond to the invitation from the American Catholic bishops to reflect in a religious way on the U.S. economy? Thinking it over for some time, Mr. Simon a month later sent out invitations to some thirty other lay Catholics, nearly all of whom agreed immediately to serve in the task. Mr. Simon accepted the burden of chairmanship, and asked Michael Novak to serve as vice-chairman. The following comments are excerpted from the Lay Commission Letter on the U.S. economy.

Points to Consider

1. What nations have raised living standards with great speed?
2. What are the causes of wealth?
3. What is the chief distinction of nations?
4. Why is the poverty of poor nations not caused by the wealth of rich nations?
5. Why is it improper to concentrate on the gap between rich and poor nations?

"Toward the Future: Catholic Social Thought and the U.S. Economy," reprinted with permission from the November, 1984 issue of *Catholicism in Crisis* (P.O. Box 495, Notre Dame, Indiana 46556).

Clearly, the chief distinction among nations is not geographical, between "North" and "South," but between profit systems and statist systems, whether traditional or socialist.

The words of Matthew 25, "Inasmuch as ye have done it unto one of the least of these my brethren, ye have done it unto me," apply as well to poor nations as to poor persons. "What you did for one, for millions, for billions, you did it to me," Pope John Paul II has commented.

In raising these passages to the level of national and international systems, however, it is crucial to understand the role of *system* in economic development. Those few societies on this planet based on private property, market systems, incentives, and the discipline of profit succeed with astonishing speed in raising up the living standards of their poor: so it has happened in recent decades in South Korea, Taiwan, Hong Kong, Singapore, Malaysia, and Japan, as earlier in Australia, New Zealand, Western Europe and the United States. Clearly, the chief distinction among nations is not geographical, between "North" and "South," but between profit systems and statist systems, whether traditional or socialist. A short time ago, several of the nations listed above stood among the poor Third World nations of the South; today they count as developed or at least very rapidly developing nations. The role of *system* in their advance is unmistakable.

Similarly, the vast "loan crisis" of recent years has dramatized beyond a doubt that the mere redistribution of financial resources may not at all assist development, in cases where internal systems frustrate such development. If nations can *borrow* fifty billion or a hundred billion dollars, and use such funds so unwisely that they do not create the new wealth to repay those funds, or even to pay the interest on them, could they not as easily lose without benefit equal or greater funds simply *given* to them? The mere influx of capital does not of itself lead to development. Immense amounts of capital, earned by hard work and savings in creative systems elsewhere, have often in recent history simply been squandered, evaporating almost without a trace. Redistribution may, or may not, help the poor. Much depends on system.

144

Uplifting the Poor

It is of profound human and Christian concern to uplift the poor universally. Frustrating such concern are statist systems of political economy which wittingly or unwittingly suppress economic creativity. If the words of Christ in Matthew 25 apply to systems, then they demand systems which actually do help the poor, not systems which so suppress economic activism as to frustrate the poor systematically.

No one can make an empirical case that "the South is getting poorer." This is not true of Australia, New Zealand, Southeast Asia, or many other places in "the South." And although many nations of the South—in Latin America and Africa, particularly— are not progressing as rapidly as they might, given more creative forms of political economy, virtually every nation without exception is experiencing undeniable signs of progress among the poor, including increased longevity, lower infant mortality, progress in literacy, higher participation in schooling at every level, and the like. Such progress could be as fast in such retarded nations as in the more rapidly developing nations, if their systems of political economy were creative instead of self-impairing.

It cannot be said empirically that the poor nations are poor because they have few natural resources, for some have many; nor because they are small, since some wealthy nations are smaller; nor because they are densely populated, since some wealthy nations are more so; nor because they were once colonies, since many of the poorest nations never were colonies and many of the wealthiest were; nor because they trade much with the richer nations, since the richer nations trade even more with one another; nor because the terms of trade for commodities are historically low, since in most cases they are not and, besides, wealth can be produced in many ways beyond the export of a few commodities. The elites of virtually every poor nation offer excuses for their poverty, preferring to blame others or hiding behind fate. It would scarcely be realistic to expect elites of the poor nations to blame themselves.

Causes of Wealth

The causes of wealth need explanation, as the causes of poverty do not, since by contemporary standards, poverty has been the condition of most peoples in most nations down through history. Unless culture and civilization intervene, poverty is humankind's natural condition, even in our own era. What is distinctive about our era is the insight that wealth can be created in a sustained way. Two hundred years after that insight was first

Source: The Freeman, 1984

expressed, the human race can now foresee the day when poverty will be universally eliminated. Even so, some will always consider themselves poor, since standards for what counts as poverty are constantly rising, and since poverty is by definition a relative condition. In Latin America, for example, it has recently become common to distinguish between the *poor* (measured by a relative financial standard) and the *destitute* (measured by a rising standard of infant mortality, nutritional sustenance, physical and mental health, longevity, economic opportunity, etc.)

What, then, are the causes of wealth? Among them, one of the chief is culture—meaning, in part, the national distribution of human capital, including habits, skills, attitudes and ambitions. The vast migrations of the twentieth century have shown that whole peoples, uprooted from one place and then transported to an undeveloped part of the world, can make even deserts bloom. The cause of wealth lies more in culture than in nature. . . .

In an unfree, uncreative political economy, the Polish priest-philosopher Jozef Tischner has written, "What good does it do when a fisherman exceeds a quota if there is no place to store the excess fish? What good does it do when people build a steel mill if the steel produced in it is more expensive and of poorer quality than the steel available on the open market? This . . . kind of betrayal consists in condemning work to senselessness."

Who can deny that under more liberating institutions of political economy the Polish people could produce greater wealth, demonstrate more effective economic dynamism, and set even for the wealthiest nations a new example of exploding creativity? Who can compare South Korea with North Korea, West Germany with East, Kenya with Ethiopia, Hong Kong with mainland China, Taiwan with Vietnam, Japan with Brazil, Australia with Argentina, and not see the difference in economic creativity that institutions of political economy can make?

Recently, Freedom House constructed a chart of all the nations, describing by type the economic system present in each, and also the relative state of political and civil liberties. The correlation between free economies and political and civil liberties is almost perfect. All the World's freest nations, and all those ranked highest in their respect for human rights, are capitalist societies. The correlation between free economies and high levels of economic development is equally close. In the real world as well as in theory, therefore, the liberal society redeems the promises both in the economic and in the political order. Capitalism seems to be a necessary, but not a sufficient, condition for political and civil liberties and also for economic development. . . .

Take, for example, the field of agriculture—the most basic of economic matters. With notable exceptions, most nations on this planet have received from the Creator sufficient arable land to be self-sufficient in food. . . .

Self-sufficiency in food is, for many poor nations, an important step towards economic development. Those systems work best in producing abundant food which most respect private property for small farmers, as well as for large; open markets and market pricing; adequate incentives for the hard and laborious work of agriculture; and wise investment and tax policies. Most democratic capitalist lands not only feed their own populations but are net exporters of food; others, such as Japan and Switzerland, specialize in mercantile or other skills in order to pay for food imports. Statist societies, whether traditionalist or socialist, have in many (if not most) cases frustrated their own farming sectors, and are net drains upon world food supplies.

Gap Between Rich and Poor

Finally, it is improper to concentrate upon "the gap" alleged to exist between poor and rich countries, rather than upon uplifting the poor within the poor countries. The latter is the criterion pointed to by Christ in Matthew 25: to feed the hungry, give drink to the thirsty, clothe the naked. Christ does not speak here about the distance between the rich and the poor, but about the real needs of the poor, which must be met. Such systematic needs can only be met by systems designed to conquer scarcity. This is the problem for which the political economy of democratic capitalism has been expressly designed. What doth it profit a nation to redistribute scarcity? The first systemic task is to produce abundance, and in such a way that the poor are quickly uplifted, as has happened in many formerly Third World nations, which deserve to be studied as models. . . .

We reject as empirically unfounded the proposition that the

wealth of some *causes* the poverty of others. We reject as false the proposition that the poverty of poor nations is caused by the wealth of richer nations. Like persons, nations are each different from every other, exhibiting inequalities along many dimensions. Yet many nations which are small, densely populated, and poor in natural resources, have developed systems of political economy which have placed them in the first rank. Chief among them, but not alone, is Japan.

Often enough, religious and moral ideas lead to the design of systems of political economy which frustrate economic activism and economic creativity. Feeding the hungry, giving drink to the thirsty, and clothing the naked means, in the long run, ceasing to frustrate the talents given every people of the planet by their Creator. Such frustration comes, most often, from the heavy hand of politics, whether in socialist or in traditional statist societies. . . .

Having seen many such cases, we thoroughly reject the view that economic benefits "trickle down" from economic heights. On the contrary, the greatest sources of new invention, new employment, and the new horizons of the future classically come from grassroots entrepreneurship, much less often than from the corporate giants. In a continental, worldwide economy, large corporations play an indispensable role. Yet a vast majority of the world's workers will depend for jobs on the flowering of millions of small enterprises. In the United States, too, the five hundred largest corporations employ only one American in eight, and they do not often serve as the cutting edge of the future. They are typically geared to providing goods and services to a very broad popular base (thus their size). By far the major source of new jobs lies in small, not large, businesses.

148

Conclusion

Economic activism characterizes a nation first at the grassroots or not at all. Since the 1960s, we have observed many developing nations attempt to energize their economies from the top down, building heavy industries under direct state control. This policy almost never works. On the contrary, those nations that have permitted and promoted economic activism at the grassroots, in the small business sector and among small farmers, have shown spectacular patterns of growth. When an entire population is economically energized from the bottom up, much faster growth ensues. Wealth does not trickle down; it wells up from below—as, most often, does economic talent.

In the task of co-creation—bringing forth from each part of creation the economic possibilities with which the Creator unequally endowed each—participation by the whole of society, from the bottom up, is in our experience, as in Catholic teaching, the most fruitful course.

ELIMINATING HUNGER IN TWO SOCIETIES

This activity may be used as an individualized study guide for students in libraries and resource centers or as a discussion catalyst in small group and classroom discussions.

Guidelines

Study the two following examples of land reform, one in a capitalist and the other in a socialist economic order. Then consider the following points for discussion.

1. Capitalism and socialism have little to do with causing the problems of hunger and starvation. Other factors such as history, population and natural wealth are more important.

2. Poor nations that adopt socialist economic systems will have the best chance to overcome hunger and poverty.

3. Hunger has been overcome in some poor nations regardless of political ideology. Communist China eliminated hunger using a socialist economy and collective farms. See examples below. Taiwan has eliminated hunger through a land reform program giving plots to small farmers within the context of a privately owned economy.

4. Both socialist and capitalist nations in Africa are failing to find solutions to the massive problems of hunger and starvation within their borders.

China's Land Reform: Example #1 (Ending hunger in a socialist nation)

After the Communists won the civil war in 1949, they took land from land owners and distributed it to peasants by forming large, publicly owned collective farms. Other reforms extended medical care, education and family planning to the rural areas. Massive hunger was eliminated, full employment now exists, abject poverty is almost gone and China has a health care system that extends to almost every person. This was done in a

150

very poor nation with a population near one billion after a great civil war, during which they were also invaded by the Japanese.

Taiwan's Land Reform: Example #2 (Ending hunger in a capitalist economy)

The reform began in 1949 after Chinese Nationalists fled to the island of Formosa (now Taiwan). The limited land resources of the island now had to support and feed a greatly increased population. All tenant-cultivated, privately-owned farmland in Taiwan was leased to those who tilled it. The next step gave landless rural workers a chance to buy land in order to increase agricultural production and raise farm income. This "land to the tiller" program took less than 10 months to complete. More than 194,800 tenants became owner-cultivators. Results were impressive in this land of privately owned factories and farms. Production greatly increased. The nation's wealth grew and great strides were made in health care, education, family planning, industrial capacity and foreign trade. Hunger was eliminated as a systemic problem. Massive amounts of U.S. aid were a key element in these reforms.

CHAPTER 5

HUNGER IN AMERICA

CHAPTER OVERVIEW

House Select Committee on Hunger

In the 1960's, a number of private, governmental, and Congressional groups investigated poverty and hunger in this country. As a result of their findings, many Americans began to see for the first time the severity of the problems encountered by the needy and underprivileged. It became clear during that time that large numbers of people in this country did not have enough to eat.

Partly in response to these findings of hunger in America, a White House conference on Food, Nutrition, and Health was convened. According to a 1970 report of the Conference, "one of the basic causes of malnutrition and hunger in the United States is poverty. Millions of Americans, of all ages and in all parts of the Nation simply do not have enough money to buy what they need in order to live healthy, productive lives."

As a result of the concern about these problems, a strategy was initiated to deal with this basic problem of poverty. This strategy focused on increasing the buying power of poor Americans so that they could purchase more food and other essentials. The primary components of this anti-poverty effort included expansion of the Food Stamp Program, increased Federal assistance for child nutrition programs, and pilot projects which employed use of food certificates for such groups as pregnant women and infants.

Throughout the decade of the 1970's, the investigation of hunger continued. Private groups, such as those funded by the Field Foundation, revisited sites covered in earlier studies. They found that the Federal anti-hunger programs had succeeded in alleviating some of the worst aspects of the hunger problem, but that some groups remained vulnerable. At the Select Committee

1984 Progress Report of the House Select Committee on Hunger, pp. 40–42.

hearing on June 25, Dr. Aaron Shirley, a Mississippi physician who had participated in two major investigations of hunger, stated that while poverty and hunger conditions exist today, the "overriding factor" contributing to the improvements which were achieved were "due to the combined benefits of the various food assistance programs put into place during the past decade."

In the 1980's, the issue of the existence of hunger in this country was once again brought to the forefront of public attention. Although the economy has been improving and the unemployment rate has dropped, poverty rates have increased and private sector anti-hunger programs have experienced great demand for food. In response to increased need due to economic factors, federal food assistance spending increased, reaching $19.4 billion in 1983. This situation—a significant federal commitment to food assistance, yet an increase in reports of hunger—illustrates the complexity of the domestic hunger problem.

Economic Factors Affecting Hunger

According to Census Bureau data, in 1983 15.2 percent of Americans—35 million people—were living in poverty. This number is the highest since 1964 and the highest rate of poverty since 1965.

For certain demographic groups, poverty rates are even higher. For example, 35.7 percent of the Black population and 28.4 percent of the Hispanic population lived in poverty in 1983. During that year, as in the preceeding few years, children fell disproportionately into poverty compared to other age groups. In the 0 to 5 age groups, 1 in 4 children lived in poverty. Nearly 1 in 2 Black children and 2 in 5 Hispanic children lived in poverty.

Some critics argue that the present method of measuring poverty, developed in the early 1960's, is outmoded and in need of revision. The current method is based on the assumption that families spend about one-third of their income on food and calculates the poverty threshold by multiplying by three the amount of money needed to purchase USDA's lowest cost diet. The majority of Federal expenditures intended to assist the low-income population are now concentrated in programs that provide in-kind or non-cash benefits. There is now a debate on how to value such benefits in calculating the poverty rate.

The availability of employment is one of the factors affecting poverty rates. Between 1973 and 1983, the nation's unemployment rate rose from 4.8 percent to 9.5 percent. In September, 1984 the overall unemployment rate had declined significantly to 7.1 percent. The number of individuals covered by unemploy-

By Web Bryant

ment insurance, however, had declined dramatically—over 70 percent—the highest percentage recorded in the history of unemployment benefits. This was partly due to increases in unemployment and changes in eligibility.

Many of those persons affected by high rates of unemployment, reductions in unemployment benefits, and fewer weeks of coverage, have been joined together to create the class today recognized as the "new poor."

Various Federal programs play a large role in determining the standard of living of the poor. Many programs have suffered a real decline in the benefit levels they provide. Reduced benefits from one program are not necessarily offset by benefits made available under another program.

The difficulties facing people in poverty have been compounded by the inflation of housing and utility costs. Utilities and housing are basic necessities which compete with food expenditures in an individual's budget. According to the U.S. Council of Economic Advisors September, 1984 report entitled "Economic Indicators", from 1974 to 1983 utility and housing costs rose 132 percent. The inflation of these costs puts a particular burden on those at or below poverty. As a result, if the poor spend more of their income on heating and shelter, they generally have less available to spend on food. It should be noted that recently inflation rates have been reduced.

Increased Demand for Emergency Food Assistance

The President's Task Force on Food Assistance found that private charitable organizations are increasing their role in the food assistance network for low-income persons. Information based on State and local surveys, Congressional hearings, and a GAO report have documented an increased demand for emergency food assistance faced by the growing network of private charitable food providers. At the July 23, 1984 San Francisco hearing, the Committee received testimony from Ms. Jan Hartsough, Chair of the Mayor's Task Force on Food and Hunger, attesting to the growth in the demand for emergency food assistance in her city. She testified that "dwindling Federal food assistance, chronic unemployment and under employment, and the high cost of living, translates into a dramatic increase in the need for local food assistance." Private sector efforts are an important way to help meet this need. Ms. Hartsough stated that the St. Vincent de Paul Society was serving approximately 25,000 meals per month in July 1984. Father Floyd Lotito and Reverend Cecil Williams—both directors of church-affiliated emergency feeding centers—testified that they had experienced a substantial growth in the number of meals that they were serving each month. It is clear that the recent recession played a role in increased demand for emergency food assistance.

A 1983 report issued by the U.S. Conference of Mayors revealed that in the eight major metropolitan areas surveyed, demand for emergency food assistance increased an average of 71 percent between 1982 and 1983. A report issued by the Texas Senate Interim Committee on Hunger and Nutrition discusses a statewide survey of 1,893 providers of emergency food assistance. According to this survey, in 1980 the service provider re-

156

ported having served 889,303 persons. "In 1983, that number had grown to 1,874,672 persons. Service in the first half of 1984 indicates that the need is still growing. Respondents report receiving over 70,000 requests for food each month and had to turn away at least 20,000 of these."

A second U.S. Conference of Mayors' report, issued in September, 1984 entitled "Survey of Human Services in the Nation's Principal Cities," reported that the demand for emergency food assistance has continued to increase during 1984 in nearly three out of four cities responding to the survey. In the 83 cities in the 27 States that responded, the existing services are unable to respond to all those requesting food assistance. The Conference of Mayors' report estimated that, on average, 25.1 percent of the demand for emergency food assistance is unmet. Furthermore, over half of these cities anticipate the demand for emergency food assistance will increase during 1985.

A portion of this increased demand for emergency food assistance may be due to increased outreach efforts by private charitable feeding programs. However, the numerous and consistent reports of this demand demonstrate that there is an increase in the need for food assistance. A 1984 report issued by the Michigan Department of Public Health states "when a family of four depending upon ADC (Michigan's Aid to Dependent Children Program) and food stamps to meet their food, shelter, clothing, and personal needs receives an income equal to 75 percent of the national poverty level, the emergency food provider is the only refuge from systematic deprivation and hunger that they have."

NO SERIOUS HUNGER PROBLEM

President's Task Force on Food Assistance

President Reagan's Task Force on Food Assistance was established on September 8, 1983, by Executive Order 12439. James Clayburn La Force, Jr., of Los Angeles, California was chosen by the President to chair the Task Force. The remaining members come from all regions of the country and from many walks of life. The organizational meeting of the Task Force was held on September 27, 1983, in Washington, D.C.

The report and recommendations of the Task Force were presented to the President on January 10, 1984, following a meeting on January 9, 1984, during which the report and recommendations were discussed and voted upon. The report was unanimously adopted by the Task force members.

Points to Consider

1. What is the medical or clinical definition of hunger?
2. How extensive is the problem of clinical hunger in America?
3. Why is it not possible to determine the extent of hunger in America?
4. What programs exist to help hungry people?

Report of the President's Task Force on Food Assistance, January, 1984, pp. 34–39.

There are intermittent national health surveys of representative samples of the entire population. These surveys have not uncovered any major problems deriving from undernutrition.

Before we can discuss the extent of hunger in America, we must first try to provide as precise a definition of the word as possible, for hunger is clearly a term that has come to mean rather different things to different people.

A Definition of Hunger:

Hunger cannot simply be equated with unemployment or poverty. To use the terms interchangeably in this way is to trivialize them; by making hunger mean everything, we make it mean nothing. Instead, we have found it useful to confine ourselves to two working definitions. The first is the scientific, clinical definition that would be used by a health professional. In this sense, hunger means the actual physiological effects of extended nutritional deprivation. The second is a necessarily looser interpretation relating more to a social phenomenon than medical results. To many Americans, hunger is also the inability, even occasionally, to obtain adequate food and nourishment. In this sense of the term, hunger can be said to be present even when there are no clinical symptoms of deprivation.

Hunger as medically defined (clinical hunger): The medical definition of hunger would be a weakened, disordered condition brought about by prolonged lack of food. In adults, the result of such hunger is a loss of weight leading eventually to reduced physical strength or impaired function. In children, the effect of prolonged lack of food is slower growth, or halted growth if the lack is severe enough, and loss of weight. In the words of Father C. Capone, the distinguished physician-nutritionist of Catholic Relief Services,

A hungry family, or a hungry community, is where there is malnutrition. When the poor appear to be adjusted to the scarcity of their resources, hunger is manifested mainly by the inferior nutritional status of certain members of the household. . . . It can easily be detected by measuring, for instance, the rate of underweight among the young children.

Physical disorders resulting from malnutrition, however, may not only be due to insufficient caloric intake; a person's diet may be deficient in certain nutrients. In contemporary America, hunger in the clinical sense of the word is unlikely to be so severe that it shows up in any more complicated symptoms than weight loss among adults, growth retardation among some children, and anemia due to certain nutrient deficiencies, especially iron.

What evidence is there of clinical hunger in our country today? The United States does not have the kind of continuous national nutritional monitoring system that could give a complete answer to that question. Still, we do have some clear indicators. First, there are intermittent national health surveys of representative samples of the entire population. These surveys have not uncovered any major problems deriving from undernutrition. While there is evidence of low intake of iron among some groups, there is no firm indication that low iron intake has become a widespread health problem. Further, there is no evidence of excessive thinness in the general population, nor is there evidence of growth problems among children.

Second, there is a continuous surveillance system in place, although not in all states, of two of the most vulnerable groups: children and pregnant women who use public health clinics. The most recent available data (which includes the first half of 1983) concerning these children indicate that the incidence of short stature has shown an overall tendency to decrease moderately over time, at least among children below two years of age, and that the incidence of anemia has probably decreased somewhat overall.

In its most recent summary evaluation of its nutrition activities, the Department of Health and Human Services stated: "For Americans, the major nutrition-related health and life-style problems do not stem from lack of nutrients. . . . In summary, our best current data suggest that, as a whole, nutrient deficiencies are not major nutrition problems for the U.S. population.

Another statistic used by some as an indicator of nutritional status is the infant mortality rate. It should be noted that this rate has been declining steadily in the U.S. over the last 30 years. This has been true for the nation as a whole, even during the last recession, although minor variations have been observed in some states. Infant mortality rates are influenced by many factors that have little or nothing to do with nutrition. Most of the decline in these rates is probably due to improved prenatal and neonatal medical care, along with better incomes, living standards, and nutrition.

We should not, however, take these clinical indicators to mean that no one suffers from undernutrition. We know that there are people who find it impossible, for financial or other reasons, to get proper attention from physicians, and among these people there are those who suffer from the physiological symptoms associated with food shortages. Therefore, some un-

160

dernutrition probably goes undetected. There are, for example, no studies of the nutritional status of the homeless, and among this very significant group there may well be important incidences of malnutrition and disease. With this possible exception, there is no evidence that widespread undernutrition is a major health problem in the United States.

Hunger as Commonly Defined: To many people hunger means not just symptoms that can be diagnosed by a physician, it bespeaks the existence of a social, not a medical, problem: a situation in which someone cannot obtain an adequate amount of food, even if the shortage is not prolonged enough to cause health problems. It is the experience of being unsatisfied, of not getting enough to eat. This, of course, is the sense in which people ordinarily use the word. It is also the sense in which the witnesses before us and many of the reports and documents we have studied have spoken of hunger. This alternative definition of hunger relates directly to our communal commitment to ensure that everyone has adequate access to food, and to the nation's endeavors to provide food assistance. And in this sense, we cannot doubt that there is hunger in America. This is the sad truth. It is easy to think of examples of this kind of hunger: chil-

161

dren who sometimes are sent to bed hungry because their parents find it impossible to provide for them; parents, especially mothers, who sometimes forego food so that their families may eat; the homeless who must depend on the largess of charity or who are forced to scavenge for food or beg; and people who do not eat properly in order that they save money to pay rent, utilities, and other bills.

Clinical hunger is relatively easy to quantify. People can be weighed and measured, and blood samples taken to indicate something about their nutritional status. But the ordinary, everyday sense in which the word hunger is used is much more difficult to identify and put a number to. How many people go hungry in the United States because their income is too low or because they are experiencing temporary financial setbacks? No one who has sincerely sought a true and responsible answer to this question has been able to provide one.

The Extent of Hunger in America:

There is no official "hunger count" to estimate the number of hungry people, and so there are no hard data available to estimate the extent of hunger directly. Those who argue that hunger is widespread and growing rely on indirect measures. The following are the main pieces of evidence used to support the claim that hunger is not only widespread but has grown worse in the last few years.

First, data have been presented to prove that there has been an increase in the number of people at or below the poverty line, and that their number is greater today than at any time in the last fifteen years. Second, there has been a significant increase in the number of people who seek food assistance. Third, there are many stories of poor families who run out of food stamps before the end of the month. Fourth, the fact that individuals eligible for food assistance programs frequently do not participate is often cited as proof that the programs are not reaching those in need.

As important as each of these separate observations seems to be, together they nevertheless do not accurately indicate the extent of the hunger problem.

To begin with, while there has undoubtedly been an increase in the number of people officially defined as poor, there are also important reasons to believe that official poverty statistics do not adequately portray the economic circumstances of low-income people, as discussed above. These technical problems of measuring poverty do not mean that there is no hunger, or that there has been no increase in the amount of poverty or hunger

162

in recent years; rather, they only mean that it is incorrect simply to point to changes in the poverty rate over this fifteen year period as an indication of the extent to which hunger has increased.

Furthermore, as incomes fall, people become eligible for food stamps and other food assistance benefits. These programs are designed to combat the hunger that is caused by unexpected reductions in income. Thus, as the size of the poverty population increases, there is a concurrent increase in the amount of public assistance.

It is true that a family suffering from inadequate access to sufficient quantities of nutritious food is most likely to be a poor family; it does not follow, however, that all poor families necessarily lack access to food of sufficient quantity or quality. In fact, there is evidence that poor families who devote relatively more of their food budget to dairy products, vegetables, and grains have little difficulty obtaining an adequate diet, including the various nutrients. . . .

Conclusion

While we have found evidence of hunger in the sense that some people have difficulty obtaining adequate access to food, we have also found that it is at present impossible to estimate the extent of that hunger. We cannot report on any indicator that will tell us by how much hunger has gone up in recent years. We have been unable to substantiate the allegation of rampant hunger. We regret our inability to document the degree of hunger caused by income limitations, for such lack of definitive, quantitative proof contributes to a climate in which policy discussions become unhelpfully heated and unsubstantiated assertions are then substituted for hard information. But we have also found that for the vast majority of low-income people, the private and public parts of the income maintenance and food assistance efforts are available and sufficient for those who take advantage of them.

Since general claims of widespread hunger can neither be positively refuted nor definitively proved, it seems likely that the issue of hunger will remain on our national policy agenda for an indefinite future. Much of the discussion generated by this issue concerns the question of how we, as a nation, set about to deal with the problem of the needy in our midst. This is a discussion that can be a healthy part of our democratic system.

25
HUNGER IN AMERICA

WIDESPREAD HUNGER IS EVIDENT IN THE U.S.

Edward M. Kennedy

Edward M. Kennedy is a United States Democratic Senator from Massachusetts. He has been a leading critic of President Reagan's policies and programs for the poor.

Points to Consider

1. Why is the President's Task Force Report a cruel joke?
2. How are Reagan Administration economic policies described?
3. What evidence is there of growing hunger in America?
4. How can Congress help fight the problem of hunger?

Edward M. Kennedy, Statement to the Joint Congressional Oversight Committee Hearings on the President's Task Force on Food Assistance, January 26, 1984, pp. 213–16.

The facts about hunger are not anecdotal. There is clear, undeniable and authoritative evidence of widespread and increasing hunger in America.

I have come here today because of my deep concern about the plight of the hungry in this country and my longstanding commitment to eliminate it.

I believe that the Task Force has failed to meet its responsibility, and I urge you to reject its attempt to place a fig leaf over the serious national problem of hunger in America.

This is the third presidential commission in a row to salute the flawed policies of the President. His MX Commission endorsed the MX missile; his Central America Commission endorsed the Administration's secret war against Nicaragua; and now his Hunger Commission reassuringly tells him what he wants to hear—that claims of widespread hunger in America cannot be "definitively proved," that the existing food assistance programs are "sufficient," and that the social safety net is intact.

To put it plainly, the Task Force report is a cruel joke on millions of our fellow citizens who continue to endure an unacceptable and unfair burden of poverty, hunger, and deprivation in this wealthy, well-fed and privileged land.

In reaching these conclusions, the Task Force has endorsed the preconceived view of Presidential Counselor, Edwin Meese, who said he had seen no definitive evidence of hunger. While the Task Force has certainly seen and knows more about hunger than Mr. Meese, it has not learned any more. Its call for an unattainable scientific precision in quantifying hunger is part of a familiar Administration strategy to ignore evidence of unfairness and injustice in America. The theme of this report is clear—see no hunger, hear no hunger, speak no hunger.

If the President had sent this crew into the desert, they would tell us that they saw some sand, but were unable to say how much.

I also reject the report's suggestion that technical problems in measuring poverty require further study before we can say with certainty that hunger and poverty are related. There is no need for further study. According to the Census Bureau, the number of people below the poverty line soared by 5 million from 1980 to 1982. The poverty gap—which measures the severity of poverty—also grew rapidly. Poor people are the most likely to be hungry people.

166

I, for one, do not believe we must identify and fingerprint the hungry before we offer them assistance. We do not need to give lie detector tests to people standing in line at the local soup kitchen before we give them a decent meal.

Hunger is not just a scientific question. It is a moral issue. And nothing in this Task Force or the Administration's policies can paper over the facts of rising hunger in America—or absolve the Administration of responsibility for the problem.

The Reagan Policies

For two decades, until Inauguration Day 1981, we had been making steady progress in the battle against hunger in America. It is true that gaps in our system of defense against encroaching poverty had begun to emerge in the late 1970s. In many states single persons and couples with children could not qualify for any welfare or Medicaid benefits, no matter how desperate their poverty. The crushing burden of inflation had reduced the purchasing power of welfare benefits by a full 30 percent over a decade.

These facts were well-known to the Reagan Administration as it prepared to submit its first budget in 1981—but the alarms that many of us in Congress tried to sound were ignored. Against the most fundamental principles of fairness and social justice, the Reagan Administration adopted a scorched earth economic program that transformed an already growing problem into a full-blown crisis of hunger in America.

Their program of lowered taxes for the rich sowed the seeds of high interest rates, and reaped the longest and deepest recession in a generation. At the same time, drastic cutbacks in medicaid and AFDC, housing allowances and energy assistance ripped apart the safety net for the poor.

And in the most unkind cut of all, the Administration took dead aim on all the important federal food assistance programs, proposing to slash a total of $9 billion from child nutrition programs over a four-year period, an overall cut of nearly 30 percent. Congress unwisely approved half of this cut which was still far too deep.

And just as the Reagan policies took hold and the budget cuts began to bite, the recession hit and the national unemployment rate grew from 7.2 percent in July 1981 to 10.8 percent in December 1982. Newly unemployed workers faced an entirely new surprise. The Administration's indiscriminate budget cuts had also cut back sharply on unemployment benefits. By mid 1983 only 38 percent of all jobless workers were receiving unemployment benefits—less than half of the percentage receiving them during the 1974–75 recession. And almost always, when unem-

167

ployment benefits were squeezed, it was nutrition that felt the pinch.

Growing Hunger

There is no doubt about the cause of the resurgence of hunger in this country. Ronald Reagan's recession and the simultaneous drastic cuts in nutrition and other social programs severed the lifeline for the millions of needy families. Forced to choose between shelter, clothing, heat and food, they gave up food.

For almost two years the Administration ignored ominous reports that more and more families were going hungry. They rejected independent studies by the Conference of Mayors and other groups, which confirmed the evidence of those reports. But when the calls of concern became all too clear, after 18 months of economic pain, what do you suppose the Administration did? They appointed a commission to tell them why there was hunger in America.

Against the inevitability of the commission's whitewash, I decided last November to investigate the problem myself. I visited San Francisco, Minneapolis, Detroit, and Pittsburgh. With Congressman Perkins, I visited a number of smaller communities in Southeastern Kentucky. I talked with people who have felt the impact of recent budget cuts in food assistance programs. I watched families with young children wait for hours to get a five pound block of cheese. I talked to doctors and nurses who are seeing and treating the effects of hunger and malnourishment in their patients. I listened to the battlefield reports from the courageous social workers and volunteers on the front line in the struggle against hunger.

Last December 22, I submitted my own report, "Going Hungry in America," to the Senate Labor Committee, detailing my conclusions and making 16 recommendations for action. In my view—shared, I believe, by anyone who has studied the problem except the Reagan Commissioners—these are three obvious points to be made:

First, the facts about hunger are not anecdotal. There is clear, undeniable and authoritative evidence of widespread and increasing hunger in America. At every location I visited, more and more people are seeking food assistance on a regular basis. The surge in requests for help began late in 1981; in most cases, those requests have doubled or even tripled over the past year. In some areas the increases are even greater.

Second, the current food assistance programs do not provide enough support to ensure an adequate diet for large numbers of

168

people. Witness after witness told us how they did not eat at all for a few days a week, or for a week or two at the end of every month. Soup kitchens and food assistance centers reported steady increase in the total number of individuals in need, and dramatic increases during the last two weeks of the month.

No evidence was presented to our forums to support the cruel and irresponsible charge that people with sufficient funds are freeloading on food pantries and soup kitchens.

Third, despite the extraordinary efforts of state, local, and volunteer groups to deal with increased demand for food, the need is far from met and the gap is growing wider. Limitations on the availability of food and inadequate distribution facilities mean that severe restrictions must be imposed on recipients. Agencies and efforts that were holding their own in the 1970s now find themselves overwhelmed by the greater demand of the 1980s.

I believe that Congress has a responsibility to act in this session to repair the holes in the safety net which have permitted the current unacceptable situation to develop. Hunger is not a new problem in America—but it is one problem we know how to solve. The landmark federal initiatives of the 1960s launched nearly two decades of progress against hunger. At a minimum, we must revise the regressive action of the past three years, and return to the path of progress. We must not permit lengthening lines at soup kitchens to become the shame of America in 1984. . . .

The Hunger Epidemic

Hunger in America is a national health epidemic.

It is our judgment that the problem of hunger in the United States is now more widespread and serious than at any time in the last ten to fifteen years. . . .

It is in fact so widespread and obvious that its existence has been documented by fifteen national studies, and even more state-level studies, during the past two years.

While no one knows the precise number of hungry Americans, available evidence indicates that up to 20,000,000 citizens may be hungry at least some period of time each month. In the 1960s, before the expansion of federal nutrition programs, hunger was a daily problem for millions of citizens. Today, evidence indicates that weaknesses in these same programs leave millions of citizens hungry several days each month, and often more. . . .

Evidence from the states and regions of the nation indicates that hunger continues to grow. . . .

Hunger does not just happen in a nation with more than enough food to feed itself and a good part of the world. Hunger occurs because policies either produce it or fail to prevent it. Today our leaders have permitted poverty in this nation to reach record levels and then cut back on programs which help our citizens endure economic hardship. As a result, America has become a "soup kitchen society," a spectre unmatched since the bread lines of the Great Depression.

Physicians Task Force on Hunger in America, 1985.

New Food Plan Needed

A realistic and affordable goal for this Congress is to adopt a new Basic Food Plan, at a level approximately 10 percent above the current Thrifty Food Plan. Leading medical and nutritional authorities have long warned that the Thrifty Food Plan is inadequate. USDA's most recent National Household Food Consumption Survey, for example, found that five of every six households whose food expenditures equalled the cost of the Thrifty Food Plan failed to obtain the Recommended Daily Allowance for basic nutrients. Unless basic benefits are increased, the present unacceptable situation will persist, and families in poverty will continue to endure the final days of each month without any food at all.

We must also make food stamp eligibility requirements less restrictive. We must increase both the overall assets limit and the shelter deduction in the food stamp program, so that the unemployed can fairly qualify for benefits. We must remove the bias against low income working parents, by permitting the deduction of child care costs and restoring the full earned income deduction. In its one positive gesture, the Task Force implicitly accepts the importance of reducing such eligibility restrictions. These reforms should be enacted into law as soon as possible. . . .

Finally, I urge the Administration to stop passing the buck to the voluntary nonprofit sector. The Task Force's not-so-subtle suggestion that voluntary efforts can fill the gap left by the President's budget cuts is false on the merits and makes a travesty of responsible and compassionate government.

The private food distribution system is already strained to the breaking point. Volunteers are overworked, the hungry are underfed; and providers are unsupplied. . . .

The 16 recommendations I have made in my report to the Senate Labor Committee have an annual cost of approximately $2.5 billion. In my view, an Administration that is bent on seeking $55 billion more dollars for defense can also find $2.5 billion more to feed the hungry.

There is no such thing as fighting hunger on the cheap. And there is no denying that recent cuts in federal food programs have exacted a fearful human cost. The recommendations I have made will put the nation back on the track toward freedom from hunger for millions of Americans who may be invisible to the White House, but who deserve a helping hand from Congress.

WHAT IS POLITICAL BIAS?

This activity may be used as an individualized study guide for students in libraries and resource centers or as a discussion catalyst in small group and classroom discussions.

Many readers are unaware that written material usually expresses an opinion or bias. The skill to read with insight and understanding requires the ability to detect different kinds of bias. Political bias, race bias, sex bias, ethnocentric bias and religious bias are five basic kinds of opinions expressed in editorials and literature that attempt to persuade. This activity will focus on political bias defined in the glossary below.

5 Kinds Of Editorial Opinion Or Bias

*sex bias—the expression of dislike for and/or feeling of superiority over a person because of gender or sexual preference

*race bias—the expression of dislike for and/or feeling of superiority over a racial group

*ethnocentric bias—the expression of a belief that one's own group, race, religion, culture or nation is superior. Ethnocentric persons judge others by their own standards and values

*political bias—the expression of opinions and attitudes about government-related issues on the local, state, national or international level

*religious bias—the expression of a religious belief or attitude

Guidelines

Read through the following statements and decide which ones represent political opinion or bias. Evaluate each statement by using the method indicated below.

Mark (P) for statements that reflect any political bias.
Mark (F) for any factual statements.
Mark (O) for statements of opinion that reflect other kinds of opinion or bias.
Mark (N) for any statements that you are not sure about.

_____ 1. A rapidly growing population will cause problems of hunger to be greater in many poor nations.

_____ 2. Foreign aid to poor nations helps the ruling elites oppress the poor and hungry.

_____ 3. Many African countries could not do without food aid from wealthy nations.

_____ 4. Rich nations have a moral obligation to help the starving people in Africa.

_____ 5. No foreign aid should be given to countries that lack a clear plan to improve conditions for the poor.

_____ 6. It is a crime for rich nations to destroy vast quantities of surplus food while millions starve every year.

_____ 7. Food aid creates dependency.

_____ 8. Nations with serious hunger problems should not permit the growth of crops for export.

_____ 9. Multinational corporations exploit the poor nations of the world.

_____10. Socialist nations should not receive long term development aid from Western countries.

_____11. The Western economies that value material abundance and luxury items are a poor role model for poor nations that must produce all they can to meet basic human needs.

_____12. Privately oriented economies that produce material abundance offer the way out of poverty for poor nations.

BIBLIOGRAPHY

World Hunger: Selected References

Brown, Lester R. Putting Food on the World's Table. **Environment,** v. 26, May 1984:15–20, 38–44.

The Causes of World Hunger. Edited by William Byron. New York, Paulist Press, 1982. 256 p.

Christensen, Cheryl, Arthur Dommen, and Peter Riley. Assessing Africa's Food Policies. **Africa Report,** v. 29, July–Aug. 1984:57–61.

Cohen, Marc J. US Food Aid to Southeast Asia, 1975–83. **Food Policy,** v. 9, May 1984:139–155.

Falcon, Walter P. Recent Food Policy Lessons from Developing Countries [With Discussion by Robert W. Herdt] **American Journal of Agricultural Economics,** v. 66, May 1984:1880–187.

Fauriol, Georges. **The Food and Agriculture Organization: A Flawed Strategy in the War Against Hunger.** Washington, Heritage Foundation, 1984. 45 p.

Food and Nutrition Bulletin. v. 1+ 1978+ Tokyo, United Nations University. Quarterly.

Food Policy. v. 1+ 1976+ Guildford, Surrey, England, Butterworth Scientific. Quarterly.

Harrison, Paul. Population, Climate and Future Food Supply. **Ambio,** v. 13, no. 3, 1984:161–167.

Hines, Colin, and Barbara Dinham. Can Agribusiness Feed Africa? **Ecologist,** v. 14, no. 2, 1984:61–66.

Huddleston, Barbara. Estimating Food Aid Needs: How Much and to Whom? **Development Digest,** v. 21, July 1983:122–134.

Isenman, Paul J., and H. W. Singer. Food Aid: Disincentive Effects and Their Policy Implications. **Economic Development and Cultural Change,** v. 25, Jan. 1977:205–237.

Johnson, D. Gale. **The World Food Situation: Developments During the 1970s and Prospects for the 1980s.** In U.S.-Japanese Agricultural Trade Relations. Edited by Emery N. Castle and Kenzo Hemmi, with Salla A. Skillings. Washington, Resources for the Future, 1982. p. 15–57.

Lewis, Clifford W. Global Food Security—A Manageable Challenge. **Development Digest,** v. 21, July 1983:106–121.

Matzke, Otto. Food Aid—Pros and Cons. **Aussenpolitik,** v. 35, no. 1, 1984:87–98.

Mellor, John W., and Richard H. Adams, Jr. Feeding the Underdeveloped World. **Chemical & Engineering News,** v. 62, Apr. 23, 1984: 32–39.

Murphy, Elaine M. **Food and Population: A Global Concern.** Washington, Population Reference Bureau, 1984. 13, 4 p.

P. L. 480: Food for Peace Program Marks Its Thirtieth Anniversary. **Foreign Agriculture,** v. 22, July 1984:14–17.

The Role of Markets in the World Food Economy. Edited by D. Gale Johnson and G. Edward Schuh. Boulder, Colo., Wesview Press, 1983. 326 p.

Scandizzo, P. L., and I. Tsakok. Food Pricing Policies in Developing Countries. **Development Digest,** v. 21, July 1983:22–32.

Walsh, John. Sahel Will Suffer Even If Rains Come. **Science,** v. 224, May 4, 1984:467–471.

Williams, Maurice J. Toward a Food Strategy for Africa. **Africa Report,** v. 28, Sept.–Oct. 1983:22–26.

Wilson, Adam. How Starvation is Fuelled in the Corridors of Power. **African Business,** no. 68, Apr. 1984:9–13.

World Food Aid Needs and Availabilities, 1984. Washington, U.S. Dept. of Agriculture, Economic Research Service, 1984. 178 p.

The World Food Situation and Prospects to 1985. Washington, U.S. Dept. of Agriculture, Economic Research Service, 1974. 90 p. (Foreign Agricultural Economic Report no. 98)

Yeaney, Timothy. **Exporting Surpluses: A Threat to Food Security?** Washington, Bread for the World, 1984. 4 p.

Hunger in America: Selected References

Berkenfield, Janet, and Janet B. Schwartz. Nutrition Intervention in the Community—The "WIC" Program. **New England Journal of Medicine,** v. 302, Mar. 6, 1980:579–581.

Boehm, William T., Paul E. Nelson, and Kathryn A. Longen. **Progress Toward Eliminating Hunger in America.** Washington, U.S. Dept. of Agriculture, 1980. 37 p. (Agricultural Economic Report, no. 446)

Boyd, Eric E. Resource Recovery: The Foodbank Movement. **Environment,** v. 25, Sept. 1983:2–5.

Demkovich, Linda E. Feeding the Young—Will the Reagan 'Safety Net' Catch the 'Truly Needy'? **National Journal,** v. 14, Apr. 10, 1982: 624–627, 629.

_____ Hunger in America—Is its Resurgence Real or Is the Evidence Exaggerated? **National Journal,** v. 15, Oct. 18, 1983:2048–2052.

_____ The Hungry Poor May Be Casualties of this Year's Battle of the Budget. **National Journal.** v. 15, Feb. 12, 1983:329–332.

Engel, Margaret, and Edward D. Sargent. Meese's Hunger Remarks Stir More Outrage Among Groups. **Washington Post,** Dec. 11, 1983:A1, A10.

Food Stamps and Hunger. New York, WNET/Thirteen, 1983. 8 p. The MacNeil/Lehrer Report, Aug. 2, 1983. Interview with Nancy Amidei of the Food Research and Action Center,

Secretary of Agriculture John Block, Senator William Armstrong, and Representative Leon Panetta.

Hunger in American Cities. [S. 1] United States Conference of Mayors, 1983. 41 p.

Kennedy, Eileen T. Evaluation of the Effect of WIC Supplemental Feeding on Birth Weight. **Journal of the American Dietetic Association,** v. 80, Mar. 1982:220–227.

Kotz, Nick. **Hunger in America: The Federal Response.** New York, The Field Foundation, 1979. 40 p.

Leepson, Marc. **Hunger in America.** Washington, Congressional Quarterly, 1983. 723–740 p. (Editorial Research Reports, 1983, v. 2, no. 12).

Morgan, Karen J., S. R. Johnson, and Jane Burt. Household Size and the Cost of Nutritionally Equivalent Diets. **American Journal of Public Health,** v. 73, May 1983:530–537.

Pear, Robert. Food Panel Urges a Slight Aid Rise in Draft Report. **New York Times,** Dec. 25, 1983:1, 27.

Ranii, Dave. Meals on Wheels: How to Turn Victory Into Defeat—And Back Into Victory. **National Journal,** v. 12, Mar. 29, 1980:522–524.

Schoen, Elin. Once Again, Hunger Troubles America. **New York Times Magazine,** Jan. 21, 1983:21–23.

Slater, Matthew D. Going Hungry on Food Stamps. **Social Policy,** v. 11, Jan.–Feb. 1981:18–24.

Srinivasan, T. N. Measuring Malnutrition. **Ceres,** v. 16, Mar. 1983: 23–27.

Tobias, Alice L., and Patricia J. Thompson. **Issues in Nutrition for the 1980s: An Ecological Perspective.** Monterey, Calif., Wadsworth Health Sciences Division, 1980. 544 p.